Ronald Reagan: Intelligence and the End of the Cold War

Historical Collection Division

The Historical Collections Division (HCD) of CIA's Information Management Services is responsible for executing the Agency's Historical Review Program. This program seeks to identify and declassify collections of documents that detail the Agency's analysis and activities relating to historically significant topics and events. HCD's goals include increasing the usability and accessibility of historical collections primarily by developing release events and partnerships to highlight each collection and make it available to the broadest audience possible.

The mission of HCD is to:

- Promote an accurate, objective understanding of the information and intelligence that has helped shape the foundation of major US policy decisions.

- Broaden access to lessons learned, presenting historical material to emphasize the scope and context of past actions.

- Improve current decision-making and analysis by facilitating reflection on the impacts and effects arising from past decisions.

- Showcase CIA's contributions to national security and provide the American public with valuable insight into the workings of its government.

- Demonstrate the CIA's commitment to the Open Government Initiative and its three core values: Transparency, Participation, and Collaboration.

The Ronald Reagan Presidential Library

As one of eleven presidential libraries administered by the National Archives and Records Administration, the Reagan Library, under the Presidential Records Act, is the repository of presidential records for President Reagan's administration. The Library's holdings include over 60 million pages of documents, over 1.6 million photographs, a half million feet of motion picture film, tens of thousands of audio and video tape, and over 40,000 artifacts. The newly renovated Museum integrates hundreds of artifacts, over half never before seen, and dozens of interactive displays. These 18 new galleries pay tribute to America's 40th president and his accomplishments by capturing his patriotic spirit, his respect for individual liberty, his belief in global democracy, and his support of economic opportunity.

Center for the Study of Intelligence

The History Staff in the CIA Center for the Study of Intelligence fosters understanding of the Agency's history and its relationship to today's intelligence challenges by communicating instructive historical insights to the CIA workforce, other US Government agencies, and the public. CIA historians research topics on all aspects of Agency activities and disseminate their knowledge through publications, courses, briefings and Web-based products. They also work with other Intelligence Community historians on publication and education projects that highlight interagency approaches to intelligence issues. Lastly, the CIA History Staff conducts an ambitious program of oral history interviews that are invaluable for preserving institutional memories that are not captured in the documentary record.

RONALD REAGAN, INTELLIGENCE, WILLIAM CASEY, AND CIA: A REAPPRAISAL

Nick Dujmovic

Ronald Reagan became the 40th president of the United States more than thirty years ago, and ever since he stepped down to return to California eight years later, historians, political scientists, and pundits of all stripes have debated the meaning of his presidency. All modern presidents undergo reappraisal after their terms in office. Dwight Eisenhower, for example, was long considered a sort of caretaker president who played a lot of golf but who was not very smart or capable; access to formerly closed administration records has changed the minds of historians, who generally consider him a president fully in charge of national policy, clear-minded, and even visionary.

Reagan has undergone a similar reappraisal. The old view, exemplified by Clark Clifford's famous characterization that Reagan was "an amiable dunce," posited Reagan as a great communicator, to be sure, but one without substance, a former actor who knew the lines others wrote for him, but intellectually an empty suit. Many commentators, especially self-described political liberals, agreed with Norman Mailer's view of Reagan as "the most ignorant president we ever had." Gore Vidal joked that the Reagan Library burned down and "both books were lost"—including the one Reagan had not finished coloring.[1] Even if these are extreme views, the perspective among many liberals, Democrats, even some Republicans, and most definitely public intellectuals (including historians) was that Reagan was never very intelligent, never very curious, and never read much; as president, he liked to watch movies and tell funny but pointless stories, delegated all hard choices, worked very little, and took lots of naps. If the Cold War largely ended on Reagan's watch, and if he oversaw an economic recovery, he was just lucky. Reagan, in the old narrative, simply could not be the architect of anything positive that happened while he was president.

That perspective has changed forever and is marked by the continually improving regard historians have for Reagan. Whereas Reagan ranked 25th among US presidents in a 1996 poll conducted by Arthur Schlesinger, Jr., among fellow historians, in 2000 a bipartisan polling of scholars ranked Reagan eighth.[2] Since 2001, the reappraisal really took off with the publication of Reagan's voluminous personal and professional writings that demonstrate he was a voracious reader, a prolific and thoughtful writer, a fully engaged mind with a clear, reasoned, and consistent philosophy.[3] More recently, scholarly analysis—some of it by former Reagan critics—of the Reagan administration record, including declassified documents, makes a convincing case that the end of the Cold War and the demise of the Soviet Union were no accidents and that Reagan deserves credit for his national security policies that led to these developments.[4] Finally, there are the illuminating Reagan diaries, which have persuaded many skeptics—including Iran-Contra prosecutor Arthur Liman—that Reagan was a thoughtful and capable president.[5]

LINGERING MYTHOLOGY ABOUT REAGAN AS INTELLIGENCE CONSUMER

The earlier assessments of Reagan and the subsequent reappraisals should matter to CIA officers because they have implications for the history of the Agency and its work. If Reagan was a lightweight who read little, was disengaged from policy, and was ignorant about matters of statecraft and national security, there are implications about how CIA produced and presented its intelligence for the Chief Executive, how much that intelligence (and therefore CIA) mattered to the Reagan administration, and how the Agency might adjust its approach to another similarly intelligence-

impaired president. The lack of a scholarly reassessment of Reagan as a user of intelligence has led to the persistence of a series of assertions consistent with the earlier general view of Reagan but similarly in need of reappraisal. These assertions are in fact overlapping, self-supporting myths about Reagan and intelligence perpetuated by prominent writers about US intelligence. There are three such myths:

Reagan was profoundly ignorant of intelligence and never cared to learn much about it. He came to the presidency, according to the author of a recent and flawed history of the Agency, knowing "little more about the CIA than what he had learned at the movies." Others have seconded this view, including former Director of Central Intelligence (DCI) Stansfield Turner, who asserts that Reagan's lack of interest in intelligence facilitated the unwarranted influence of DCI William Casey on the president and on policy.[6]

Reagan was not much of a reader of intelligence because he tended to read little of anything, especially material (like intelligence) with which he was not already familiar or interested in. Casey himself initially took this stance—saying to an aide, "If you can't give it to him in one paragraph, forget it"—before he learned otherwise. Former DCI Turner says that Reagan paid little attention to CIA products like the President's Daily Brief (PDB), citing Vice President George Bush's statement that Reagan read intelligence only "at his leisure."[7] Others go so far as to assert that Reagan generally read no intelligence estimates or assessments of any kind; a highly regarded history of CIA's work in Afghanistan from the Reagan years to the 9/11 attacks asserts that the Agency learned early that "Reagan was not much of a reader" and that detailed written intelligence "rarely reached his desk."[8] Variants on the theme that Reagan read little or no intelligence include the notion that Reagan's PDB was unusually short (implicitly by the standards of other presidents) to encourage his reading it or that Reagan's PDB was orally briefed to him so he would not have to read it.[9]

Because Reagan was not a reader, he preferred to watch intelligence videos and films made for him in lieu of traditional printed intelligence products. This myth is supported by Reagan's purported preference as a former career actor in films and television and by the old perspective of Reagan's simple-mindedness. One widely quoted intelligence scholar (a former CIA analyst) asserts that CIA managers made sure to give the president his intelligence in the form he preferred—images rather than text.[10] Another sniffed that Reagan "wanted a show" instead of traditional printed reports, so he received "intelligence briefings in video format in which predigested facts were arranged like decorations on a cake. . . a mode of presentation [that] blurred any distinction between fact and judgment, intelligence and advertising, reality and artist's conception."[11] A recent (2009) study of intelligence analysis by a respected Washington think tank asserts that the PDB as prepared for Reagan conformed to his preferences, which were for "simple briefings" and "audio-visual presentations."[12]

These three Reagan intelligence myths are consistent with the old interpretation of Reagan the insubstantial president but directly conflict with the more recent evidence that indicates Reagan was a capable and engaged Chief Executive. In any case, these myths persist, probably from a lack of published evidence specifically covering Reagan's use of intelligence combined with a partisanship that blinds some intelligence writers to the facts that have come to light. This paper will present new intelligence-specific findings on Reagan that will refute these myths.

REAGAN'S UNDERSTANDING OF INTELLIGENCE BEFORE HIS PRESIDENCY

Much—probably too much—has been made of Reagan's acting career and its alleged influence on his substantive knowledge of intelligence and national security matters. Even the widely esteemed Professor Christopher Andrew of Cambridge University opens his otherwise superb discussion of US intelligence in the Reagan years with the observation that a third of the films Reagan made in the late 1930s and early 1940s dealt with national security threats; Andrew considers especially telling the four "Brass Bancroft" films in which Reagan starred as Secret Service Agent J-24. More significant, however, was Reagan's wartime service making films for Army Air Corps intelligence, particularly those films used for briefing pilots and bombardiers before their Pacific war missions. The intelligence unit to which Reagan was assigned used prewar photographs and intelligence reports to construct large scale models of targets, over which a moving camera would film; Reagan would then record a narration telling the pilots and bombardiers what they were seeing and when to release their payloads.[13] Reagan thereby had direct experience in the production of an overhead imagery product that had operational value.

The story of Reagan's struggle with Hollywood's leftists in the late 1940s is well known.[14] After World War II, Reagan rose to the leadership of the Screen Actors Guild (SAG), which was facing an attempted takeover by a stealth Communist faction and which had to deal with Communist-inspired labor unrest. Reagan successfully fought the attempts of the Communists to gain influence in SAG, and he persuaded union members to cross picket lines at Communist-organized studio strikes. He was threatened personally for his efforts—an anonymous caller warned he would have acid splashed into his face—and he acquired and started carrying a handgun. He became a secret informant for the FBI on suspected Communists and their activities, but publicly Reagan named no names and asserted that the film industry could handle the problem itself without government intervention. These experiences are invariably described—apparently accurately, given Reagan's subsequent move into politics—as hugely influential on a formerly politically naïve young actor, in particular by shaping his anti-Communist ideology. But these experiences were relevant also to Reagan's understanding of intelligence. Through

them Reagan learned something about secret groups undertaking clandestine activities, the challenges of working against ideologically driven adversaries, and the value of intelligence sources with access (in this case, himself).[15]

Reagan lent his celebrity support during 1951 and 1952 for the "Crusade for Freedom," a fundraising campaign to benefit Radio Free Europe (RFE). It remains unclear whether Reagan at the time knew he was participating in one of CIA's most significant Cold War influence programs. His involvement was sparked in September 1950, when Reagan, in his capacity as SAG president, wrote to the chairman of the Crusade for Freedom, retired general Lucius Clay, pledging the support of the more than 8,000 members of SAG: "We offer you our complete support in this great counter-offensive against Communist lies and treachery." In his televised appeals, Reagan modestly introduced himself—he was a well known film star at the time—and concluded by saying "The Crusade for Freedom is your chance, and mine, to fight Communism. Join today." Reagan at the time might well have suspected US government involvement in the Crusade for Freedom, since its operating entity, the National Committee for a Free Europe, boasted Allen Dulles in its leadership (Dulles had not yet joined CIA but was well known as a former OSS spymaster). As a well connected Hollywood star, he could hardly have failed to notice when syndicated columnist Drew Pearson publicized the CIA backing of RFE in March 1953, or when another media personality, Fulton Lewis, attacked RFE's CIA connection during 1957-58 in his radio shows and syndicated columns for King Features.[16] Whether or not Reagan in the 1950s knew about CIA's sponsorship of RFE, it probably would not have mattered to him, but in any case he would have found out when it was officially disclosed in 1971, after which it was publicly funded. Reagan never disavowed his participation in a covert "hearts and minds" operation that was consistent with his visceral anti-Communist beliefs, nor did he ever suggest he had been duped.

Reagan's later emphasis on the importance of counterespionage as a vital pillar of intelligence stems in part from his time as governor of California from 1967 to 1975. Reagan had a cooperative, even warm relationship with the FBI, which opened a field office in Sacramento not long after Reagan was first inaugurated. Reagan's staff informed the Bureau that the Governor "would be grateful for any information [regarding] future demonstrations" at the Berkeley campus of the University of California—a major political challenge for Reagan at the time—and other types of "subversion." Reagan sent a warm personal letter to FBI director J. Edgar Hoover praising the Bureau for its "continuing fight against crime and subversion" and pledging his help. At the bottom of the letter, Reagan wrote in his own hand, "P.S. I've just always felt better knowing your men are around." Declassified FBI documents show that Reagan received at least 19 discrete and credible threats against him during his eight years as governor, many of which were passed to him.[17]

Reagan's tenure as governor also provided direct experience regarding classified material and security clearances, since his duties included oversight of Lawrence Livermore National Laboratory—a national resource for nuclear research—which required Reagan to hold a "Q" clearance granted by the Atomic Energy Commission.[18]

THE ROCKEFELLER COMMISSION, JANUARY – JUNE 1975

Reagan's most formative and direct pre-presidential experience of CIA and intelligence undoubtedly was his participation in 1975 as a member of the President's Commission on CIA Activities within the United States, better known informally as the Rockefeller Commission after its chairman, Vice President of the United States Nelson Rockefeller. President Gerald Ford created the commission on 4 January 1975 to investigate allegations, published in the New York Times the previous month, that the Agency had illegally spied on domestic groups, especially the anti-war movement, during the presidencies of Lyndon Johnson and Richard Nixon. Reagan at the time was within days of stepping down after two terms as governor, and he was named along with a bipartisan mix of career public servants that included former cabinet secretaries, a former chairman of the Joint Chiefs of Staff, and leaders in labor and education. The White House, in announcing the appointments, noted that the eight members (including Rockefeller) were chosen because they were respected citizens with no previous connections with CIA—though certainly most had some knowledge of intelligence.[19]

The FBI in January 1975 interviewed dozens of Reagan's friends, associates, colleagues, and others pursuant to its background investigation of Reagan before he could participate on the Rockefeller Commission. Documents from Reagan's FBI file indicates that almost all those interviewed highly recommended Reagan for the position, praising his intelligence, loyalty, honor, and dedication, but there were a few exceptions, mostly among Reagan's former political rivals. Jesse Unruh, the former speaker of the California Assembly (whom Reagan had defeated in his reelection campaign in 1970) considered Reagan unqualified for any government position because of his lack of "compassion" for people; former California governor Edmund "Pat" Brown said that Reagan was "out of touch with the common man" and that his "overemphasis" on security and law enforcement "would raise a question of possible bias in favor of the CIA"; US Senator Alan Cranston challenged Reagan's capabilities for the position on the grounds that he was" insufficiently concerned about civil liberties." None of Reagan's critics, however, expressed the opinion that he was ignorant about intelligence.[20]

At the Commission's first meeting in the Vice President's office on 13 January 1975, Reagan informed Rockefeller that his busy schedule—booked full over several months with speaking engagements and taping sessions for his radio commentaries—meant that he would have to miss

some meetings. Rockefeller accepted Reagan's absences on the condition that he read the transcripts of the meetings he would miss. Reagan missed the next four meetings due to these previous commitments and because of the difficulty commuting from California to Washington, where the Commission met. Following unfavorable media reports and critical editorials in February, Reagan offered to step down from the Commission, an offer Rockefeller refused, again on the basis of Reagan's ability to read the transcripts.[21] Reagan ended up attending eleven of the Commission's 26 sessions over the next six months, which irritated Rockefeller, who as a liberal Republican was a political rival of Reagan's.[22] According to Rockefeller's counsel at the time, Peter Wallison, Rockefeller "regarded Reagan as a lightweight who was not taking his responsibilities seriously." Scholarly critics ever since, when they mention Reagan's participation in the Commission at all, point to his poor attendance record as evidence that Reagan was not very interested in CIA and intelligence.[23]

Testimony from participants and witnesses, however, paints a different picture. Reagan was not only substantively engaged, he emerged as a leader within the Commission. He did miss many meetings, especially in the beginning, but his absences were not due to lack of interest or ability. Former Commission staff counsel Marvin Gray remembers that "frankly, he didn't miss very much in those first stages. It wasn't bad judgment on his part to miss those first meetings, when we were just getting organized and before we really got started." Wallison recounts that Reagan, when he attended, listened attentively to the proceedings. The Commission's senior counsel, David Belin—who has been publicly critical of Reagan—has written that Reagan kept himself informed through his absences; Belin noted that "I was able to keep him advised on all key questions." According to Belin, Reagan showed leadership in disagreeing with Rockefeller's views on two issues: whether the Commission should investigate CIA assassination plots against foreign leaders, and whether the work of the Commission should be sealed from public access for five years. Rockefeller opposed the first and advocated the second. Reagan took the position that the Commission should look into assassination plots and opposed Rockefeller's proposal for the five-year moratorium. Reagan's position on both issues influenced others on the Commission and became the majority view. On the matter of assassinations, the Commission ran out of time to conduct a full investigation, electing to transfer its materials on the subject to the President (who sent them to the ongoing Senate investigation known as the Church Committee), while Reagan's view on openness helped lead to the June 1975 unclassified publication of the Commission's report.[24]

Testimony about the drafting of the report itself provides more insight into the question of Reagan's understanding of complex issues such as intelligence. "Unlike other commissions where the commissioners merely sign off on what the staff has written," Gray noted, "for the Rockefeller Commission the members were very involved in drafting the report." Reagan, Gray said, played an important role in drafting the report: "I was surprised by how Ronald Reagan came up with a point of view and language that allowed the Commission, often divided on issues, to compromise."[25]

Gray was not alone in his newfound appreciation for Reagan's abilities. Wallison, at the time a "Rockefeller Republican" who initially shared his boss's disdain for Reagan, quickly changed his mind: "As the commission began to draft its report . . . a contributing Reagan emerged. . . Rockefeller was not an analytical or critical thinker [and] was not able to offer much leadership in the actual drafting of the report."[26]

> For a while the commission seemed unable to develop a generally acceptable formulation of its views. As the discussions went on inconclusively, Reagan started to write on a yellow legal pad that he brought with him. At first I thought he was simply taking notes. Then, on several occasions, when the discussion flagged, he would say something like "How does this sound, fellas?" and would read aloud what he had written. His draft language was usually a succinct summary of the principal issues in the discussion and a sensible way to address them. Often, the commission found that they could agree with his proposal, which went directly into the report. . . Among a group of gifted and famous men, in the setting of the Commission on CIA Activities in the United States, Reagan was a standout.

Wallison remembers his amazement that Reagan "was really able to digest a lot of very complicated stuff [and] to write it all down in a logical order, in a smoothly flowing set of paragraphs that he then read off to the Commission members. It summarized for them and for all of the rest of us what we had heard." This was so impressive, Wallison writes, because Reagan went beyond the understanding of complex issues to being capable of accurately describing them—"adopting actual words to describe these concepts can be quite difficult. . . if one's understanding is limited, it is difficult to choose the right words. Having a sufficient mastery of the subject matter to prescribe a solution is harder still. Reagan more than met these standards." Wallison's account is confirmed by Commission member Douglas Dillon, a former Treasury secretary for Presidents Kennedy and Johnson, who recounted that Reagan's intervention ended an "impasse" among the commissioners and who was surprised by the ease with which Reagan pulled it off.[27]

CIA's critics and congressional Democrats have long derided the Rockefeller Commission's findings as a "whitewash," but it was far from that. The report Reagan helped bring to life was critical of CIA. It described at length the domestic activities revealed by the New York Times and additionally uncovered a few other abuses for the first time, such as the testing of LSD on unwitting Americans, one of whom had committed suicide.[28] As a result of his membership on the Rockefeller Commission and his leading role in drafting its final report, Reagan was well grounded on both the fun-

damentals and specifics of CIA's missions, activities, and responsibilities as well as its organization, oversight, and legal and regulatory constraints.

In the immediate wake of his Commission experience, Reagan—who philosophically was suspicious of encroachments of the federal government on individual liberty—enthusiastically defended the mission of intelligence in keeping the nation secure. As Congress continued its own investigations of US intelligence activities, Reagan publicly called for an end to ongoing congressional inquiries (the Senate's Church Committee and the House's Pike Committee investigations), saying that the Rockefeller Commission report satisfied the public's need to know, that Congress was approaching the subject with "an open mouth and a closed mind," and that further investigation would harm CIA's ability "to protect the security of this country."[29]

REAGAN'S DEVELOPING VIEWS ON INTELLIGENCE, 1975-1979

Reagan put the knowledge he acquired from his membership on the Rockefeller Commission to good use during his "wilderness period" from January 1975, when he stepped down as California's governor, to October 1979, as he was preparing to announce his candidacy for the Republican nomination for president. During this period, Reagan wrote and delivered hundreds of commentaries for his syndicated radio spot that ran five days a week; he also drafted opinion pieces, private letters, and public remarks.[30] In these writings, Reagan commented on a broad range of foreign, national security, and domestic topics, including intelligence and CIA. Early on, in a radio broadcast he titled "CIA Commission," Reagan in August 1975 highlighted his service on the Rockefeller Commission and emphasized that, though instances of CIA domestic espionage were found, it did not constitute "massive" spying as reported in the media, the misdeeds were "scattered over a 28-year period," and CIA had long ago corrected them. Reagan reiterated his concern that congressional investigations were assuming the character of "witch hunting" and threatened "inestimable harm" to CIA's ability to gather intelligence. "There is no doubt," Reagan warned, that intelligence sources worldwide "have been frightened into silence" and that CIA officer themselves were now less likely to take risks.[31]

The need for secrecy in intelligence and the potential harm of publicity is a frequent theme in Reagan's writings and public statements during this period, frequently coupled with statements of enthusiasm for the work of US intelligence officers and of the overall need for a strong intelligence posture to protect US national security in a perilous world. Many of Reagan's radio commentaries were mostly or entirely devoted to the subject of intelligence: "CIA Commission" (August 1975); "Secret Service" (October 1975); "Glomar Explorer" (November 1976); "Intelligence" (June 1977); "Spies" (April 1978); "Intelligence and the Media" (October 1978); "Counterintelligence" (January 1979); "CIA"

(March 1979). Many more touched on intelligence subjects, sometimes to make a broader political point, sometimes for their own sake. Americans have more to fear, Reagan often said, from domestic regulatory agencies like the Internal Revenue Service and the Occupational Safety and Health Administration than from intelligence agencies like CIA or the FBI. The threat from Soviet expansionism, terror, and domestic subversion required robust US capabilities in intelligence collection—Reagan highlighted the need for human and technical collection alike—as well as in counterintelligence. Addressing well publicized intelligence issues of the 1970s, Reagan advocated allowing journalists to volunteer as intelligence sources but declared "the US should not be involved in assassination plots." He strongly favored covert action programs that might lead to freedom for people living under Communist regimes, and he supported FBI surveillance and infiltration of domestic extremist groups. Not leaving any major intelligence function untreated, Reagan cited intelligence analysis to inform his radio audience of the threat from the North Korean military or from Soviet strategic weapons. He even praised liaison relationships for the intelligence they could provide while US agencies were "hamstrung" by investigations.[32]

Beginning in 1977, Reagan began to increase his public advocacy for the work of US intelligence agencies as he stepped up his criticism of President Jimmy Carter, who had called CIA one of the three "national disgraces" (along with Vietnam and Watergate) during his presidential campaign. Reagan had supported George H.W. Bush when President Ford had nominated him as DCI in early 1976, and a year later Reagan declared that Bush should remain DCI because of his success in rebuilding CIA's morale. Reagan was reportedly horrified at Carter's nomination of former Kennedy speechwriter Ted Sorensen as DCI. "We need someone who would be devoted to an effective CIA" and who recognizes the danger posed by the Soviet military buildup so that the US would not be "flying blind in a dangerous world." "Let's stop the sniping and the propaganda and the historical revisionism," Reagan said, "and let the CIA and other intelligence agencies do their job."[33]

The evidence of Reagan's pre-presidential experiences demonstrate that the man elected in November 1980 to be the 40th President of the United States had a broad knowledge of and deep appreciation for intelligence and CIA and that he had reflected on the wide range of intelligence issues, including its proper missions and activities.

THE TRANSITION PERIOD: REAGAN AS FIRST CUSTOMER-ELECT

In addition to the record of Reagan's pre-presidential knowledge of intelligence issues, CIA's experience with Ronald Reagan during the three-month period between the election of 1980 and his inauguration undermines the myth that Reagan was neither interested in intelligence

nor read much of it. Proponents of this view (see footnotes 6-9) ignore or are unaccountably unaware of the unclassified 1997 Studies in Intelligence article on the subject, prepared by the PDB briefers for the President-elect, Richard Kerr and Peter Dixon Davis.[34] Kerr and Davis recount that senior CIA officials had low expectations of Reagan as a reader of intelligence, given his lack of foreign policy experience and the presumption that his mind was made up on many issues, but even so they boldly asked George H.W. Bush, the Vice President-elect and former DCI, to urge Reagan to accept daily briefings while he remained in California before the inauguration. Bush used his influence and CIA experience to make the case, Reagan agreed, and the briefings were arranged.

Kerr and Davis's article deals mostly with the process and logistical challenges in getting the PDB to the President-elect in California, but it also reveals a Reagan who was, contrary to the persistent stereotype, a careful, studious, and diligent reader of intelligence, who went over intelligence items "deliberately and with considerable concentration," who asked questions and "showed no impatience or disdain with analysis that presented a different view" from his own; "the door seemed to be open to new ideas, even if they were not welcome or necessarily accepted." Because of Reagan's "willingness and patience in reading items," Kerr and Davis were frank in pointing out where the factual basis of an article was weak or the analysis was superficial. For his part, Reagan expressed particular interest in, and asked more questions about, certain subjects of high priority to him, particularly on Middle East issues and the Iran hostage situation: "he absorbed whatever raw and finished intelligence we were able to offer on the subject."[35]

CIA records confirm this public account and enhance the picture of a President-elect deeply engaged with the global issues of the day that the Agency covered.[36] Reagan showed particular interest in reports of Soviet consumer frustration and economic troubles, especially in agriculture; he was "very interested and attentive" to strategic arms control issues; he showed "keen interest" in reporting on foreign leaders' attitudes and plans regarding the incoming administration; he was "very interested in and somewhat concerned over" Soviet strategic weapons capabilities and deployments, as well as the Polish situation. A typical observation was "Reagan read through the book slowly and carefully, clearly very interested, concerned, and receptive to material" that included additional background papers on selected countries and issues, often sparked by Reagan's questions. On feeding Reagan supplementary reports, Davis once commented "What a willing customer!" Briefings did not occur every day due to the competing demands placed on the President-elect's time and attention, but when there was a gap between briefings, Reagan carefully read the PDBs he had missed. In all, Reagan received 27 CIA briefings between 22 November 1980 and 14 January 1981, more than half the working days of that period, which included major holidays.

PRESIDENT REAGAN AS AN INTELLIGENCE CONSUMER

Reagan's inner circle decided to end CIA's direct daily briefing of the President after the inauguration in favor of a briefing by his national security advisor and selected staff—a briefing that would include the PDB but without a CIA officer present.[37] This deprived the Agency of further direct observation of Reagan's reading intelligence as President, so we have to turn to other evidence to ascertain the degree to which Reagan read intelligence.

There is much indirect evidence that Reagan habitually read intelligence analysis from CIA. The fact that CIA reports of current interest to the administration were often routed to "PDB Principals"—including the President—indicates this material went to him, and DCI Casey often would attach personal cover notes to Reagan on reports he thought the President should read, which suggests Casey had reason to believe Reagan read them.[38] It is reasonable to assume that Reagan read CIA reports relevant to current policy issues. National security advisors would request from CIA—often directly through the DCI—analysis on relevant issues specifically for the President's reading, and often ahead of a major policy decision. For example, a CIA assessment emphasizing Nicaragua's importance to Moscow's aim to increase its influence in Latin America at the expense of the United States was disseminated just days before Reagan signed a new covert action finding on 1 December 1986 authorizing CIA to "conduct paramilitary operations against Nicaragua."[39] White House policy meetings of the NSC or the smaller National Security Policy Group (NSPG), over which Reagan also presided, were often preceded by distribution of relevant intelligence reports that served as the basis of discussion, for example, on the Soviet Union's reliance on Western trade, the Siberian oil pipeline, or the status of Soviet ballistic missile defenses.[40]

Senior members of Reagan's administration also have recounted that the President read and took seriously daily intelligence reports as well as longer intelligence assessments such as National Intelligence Estimates (NIEs). Former Secretary of State George Shultz, former presidential counselor Edwin Meese, former national security advisor Richard Allen, and former NSC senior staffer Richard Pipes have stated that Reagan regularly read and wanted to read intelligence assessments. Another former national security advisor, Robert McFarlane, recalls that Reagan enthusiastically read and marked up intelligence documents, and even recommended them to senior administration officials. Allen regularly prepared, as he put it, a "weekend reading assignment" on national security and foreign policy issues for the President to read at Camp David or on trips, and the package included intelligence assessments Allen selected for him. Reagan faithfully and regularly worked through the thick stack of his "homework," as his diary entries call his after-hours and weekend reading—Allen said Reagan read it all—to the point that Nancy Reagan told the President's aide Michael Deaver that the reading should be cut back at least 75 percent. Allen refused, saying he, not Deaver,

was responsible for keeping the President informed on national security and foreign affairs, and Reagan kept doing his "homework."[41]

Reagan also took the initiative when it came to his intelligence reading. In addition to the tasking DCI Casey would give to the DI for analysis of interest to the President, Reagan himself would occasionally commission an intelligence assessment, as when he requested an interagency perspective on foreign involvement in Grenada after the US military's operation there in October 1983.[42] More often, however, Reagan would request specific reports from a menu of options placed before him. Beginning early in his administration, the PDB—generally the Saturday book—would contain an extra page titled "Selected Reports," by which CIA provided titles and brief summaries of intelligence analysis that CIA had published the previous week and that were available in full if desired. Of the five to seven reports listed, Reagan often would select one to three full reports by circling the item or placing a check mark next to it, or both, and writing something like "order for me, please." On one "Selects" page in September 1982, Reagan marked a particular report with the words, "Send me another copy." It is not known why he needed another copy, but the 11-page report he wanted (again) was not light reading but was rather a rather complicated treatment of a subtle technical point regarding an arms control matter.[43]

Thus far the evidence for Reagan as a reader of intelligence has been indirect because it is not in the nature of printed text on paper to reveal what particular eyes read it—the act of reading itself leaves no traces. Reagan, however, often would initial papers that he had read, perhaps as a personal way of keeping track of his progress working through a pile of "homework," or perhaps as a signal to aides that he had done the reading they had requested. In any case, we have several examples of Reagan's initialing intelligence products, sometimes also writing the date he had read the material (sometimes also a secretary would also stamp the document "The President has seen"). Reagan initialed, for example, Richard Allen's cover memo on a special NIE that explained how Soviet military strength was largely dependent on Western trade; Allen had called this estimate to the President's attention as "extremely important." Likewise, Reagan initialed Robert McFarlane's cover memo on CIA's first major assessment of Gorbachev in June 1985. The initials "RR" are prominent on the cover of an NIE on China provided to him in October 1983 and on a Soviet strategic nuclear NIE in April 1985. We also have two of the monthly global threat updates from the NIC, from December 1984 and January 1985, that Reagan initialed and dated.[44] These are a handful of examples scattered over a few years, to be sure, but they were found—and could only be found—by happenstance. There is no discrete collection of, and no way to specifically search for, intelligence products—classified or declassified—with Reagan's distinctive "RR" inscribed thereon. These limitations suggest that the examples found thus far of Reagan's reading and initialing intelligence are not isolated instances but indicative of a frequent practice of his.

REAGAN AND THE PDB

No such limitations hindered research into Reagan's reading of the PDB. Then as now, the President's copy of the PDB was returned, with extremely rare exceptions, to CIA, where it was filed and archived. If Reagan read the PDB, and if he marked it as a reader, we should have the evidence. As it turns out, that evidence exists, but interpreting it requires context.

That Reagan read the PDB regularly is established by those who served him closely. Richard Allen says that Reagan read the PDB "nearly every day," and Edwin Meese said the President read the PDB "assiduously." George Shultz disliked CIA analysis but read the PDB every day because he knew the President was reading it.[45] Robert Kimmitt, an NSC staffer during the Reagan administration (and later Under Secretary of State for Political Affairs), helped prepare the daily package of the PDB and other national security readings for Reagan. In an interview with CIA's Center for the Study of Intelligence, Kimmitt was asked about Reagan and the PDB.

> My view is that he probably read the PDB page-for-page, word-for-word every day. Because I can just think of so many occasions when issues would come up, that he would be on top of, that you could only have done it if you'd been keeping up with developments. . . whatever the sort of common knowledge is about President Reagan—his intelligence, his attentiveness, and all the rest—he was the most incredible listener, and fact and information absorber, I ever viewed at that level.[46]

I was able to review the President's copy of the PDB for each day it was published from January 1981 through April 1984, about forty percent of his presidency, or about one thousand PDBs. The first conclusion one can draw is that this is a lot of intelligence reading. This body of intelligence that his closest advisors say he read regularly consists of upwards of 10,000 pages just for this period, or some 25,000 cumulative pages of daily intelligence reading for Reagan's entire presidency.[47]

The second conclusion is that the individual PDBs prepared for Reagan were not thin, as some suggest. Christopher Andrew, in his otherwise indispensable For the President's Eyes Only (1995), suggests Reagan was not much of a reader. Citing an "unattributable interview" with a "senior CIA analyst," Andrew says the typical PDB for Reagan comprised four 150-word main stories plus "a few shorter pieces and the occasional anecdote," giving the impression that Reagan could not bother to read more than 700 or 800 words in his daily intelligence report.[48]

If one reviews an actual "typical PDB" prepared for Reagan, however, the picture is quite different. A typical PDB for President Reagan actually comprised about 1600 to 1800

words or more, not 700 or 800. My personal observation as a former PDB editor during 1997-2000 is that the PDBs prepared for Ronald Reagan in the 1980s were very much alike in format and length to those I helped prepare for President Bill Clinton in the late 1990s.

But did Reagan provide tangible evidence of his reading the PDB? Robert Kimmitt, though he believes Reagan read the PDB, says there is no proof because Reagan did not write anything on it.[49] Kimmitt's impression is incorrect, for the review of the PDBs produced for Reagan shows that he did in fact write or mark upon it, but not as frequently as might be expected (or hoped)—less than ten percent of the time. Asked about the relative lack of presidential markings on Reagan's copy of the PDB, Richard Allen revealed that he advised Reagan not to write on it:

> Early on, I suggested the President not write on the PDB too frequently, as I did not know precisely who would be assessing his particular copy. . . It would not have been too clever to push down into any bureaucracy, mine [i.e. the NSC staff] or yours [CIA], any comments that could be quoted by status seekers, leakers, or for any other purpose.

Even so, Allen recounted that he was "sure" that Reagan did write occasionally on the PDB, as he had requested Reagan to indicate which PDB articles were of particular interest and which should be followed by tasking for additional analysis.[50]

Reagan did write occasionally on his copy of the PDB in often illuminating ways—they are sporadic but telling. The range includes everything from check marks to complete sentences. Most frequently, Reagan used a whole gamut of "non-verbal reader's marks" that confirm what CIA's pre-inaugural PDB briefers found—that he was a careful, interested reader. The underlining, brackets (and double brackets), circling of items, and exclamation points (sometimes two or three) are marks of a reader, not a briefer (who would underline or highlight key sentences, as Allen and his successor William Clark did intermittently), and comparison with Reagan's distinctive writing indicates they are in his hand.

Reagan would write words on his PDB to express different things. Sometimes he indicated his desire for more analysis with "And?" at the end of a paragraph. On one piece that concluded with a summary of CIA's collection efforts on the problem, he wrote "but what else?" Reagan mused on whether a particular country would violate an arms control treaty by writing "breakout?" on an article covering the issue.

On occasion Reagan would tell CIA how he liked his intelligence presented. Items in the PDB normally ended with a horizontal line across the page. Once, when the line was omitted, Reagan drew it in and wrote, "I like line after item ends." More often, however, Reagan was reacting to the substance of the intelligence provided. On a piece describing the movement of Soviet military forces to a client state, Reagan summed up the figures himself and wrote "5000 SOVIETS" in the margin. On a graphic of a Soviet mobile missile launcher, he scrawled "SCUD." Reagan also considered policy issues when reading the PDB. At a time when his administration was following developments in a certain country undergoing political and social upheaval while his NSC was discussing policy alternatives, Reagan circled a relevant item on that country and wrote "This may become an incident sufficient to" and then spelled out a particular policy option.

In one case, Reagan demonstrated how closely he read his intelligence by catching a mistake on the part of the PDB editor. He was reading a two-page Article on Soviet arms control. In the fourth paragraph on the first page, the analysis said "The Soviets believe" so and so. In the middle of the second page, another country's leaders were said to believe the same thing, "unlike the Soviets." Reagan wrote, "Is this a misprint? See previous page." He then underlined both passages. From my personal experience editing the PDB, this must have been horrifying for the PDB editorial staff. It is one thing to discover after the fact that a contradiction has made it into the President's book, but for the President himself to point out the mistake must have been professionally scandalous. Perhaps the discomfort of CIA editors, however, would be exceeded by the confusion of those intelligence scholars and other writers who assert that Reagan did not pay much attention to intelligence.

WHAT HAPPENED TO ALL OF REAGAN'S VIDEOS

The recurrent myth about Reagan's reliance on videos for his consumption of intelligence can finally be laid to rest. I requested a search for all videos produced from 1981 through 1988, and I spoke with the officer, now retired, who supervised the unit producing those videos during 1981-86. There are no PDB videos because none were made. A daily or even a weekly PDB video would have been impossible, given the minimum production time of three to four weeks for each video. At that time, daily short deadline productions were out of the question.

Although PDB videos were never made, a number of CIA video presentations were made specifically for Reagan. There is no doubt that Reagan found these intelligence videos useful. On one occasion, Reagan recorded in his diary watching "a classified film" on a particular leader: "These films are good preparation. . . They give you a sense of having met him before." Three of the intelligence videos are scene-setters or advanced travelogues for presidential trips, including side travel by Mrs. Reagan, but the majority by far were substantive and issue-specific. Reagan indicated how much he appreciated these videos when he recorded his viewing of one on 14 October 1982: "Back at the W.H. saw a 20 min. C.I.A. movie on the Soviet Space Prog[ram]. They are much further ahead than most people realize and their main effort has been military."[51] But no one should

exaggerate the significance of the video intelligence Reagan consumed, especially compared with the great quantities of printed intelligence he read. If Reagan watched every single video prepared for him during his presidency, he would have watched an average of one video every two months.

A final problem for the proponents of the view that Reagan or his advisors expected or demanded videos for the President is the fact that the impetus came from CIA, not from the White House. CIA suggested to the White House in the summer of 1981 that the videos, already in production as an in-house effort, might be helpful for Reagan. With DCI William Casey's approval and support, the first video for Reagan was delivered in September 1981.[52] Feedback from the White House was invariably good, and there were increasing requests for more videos from around the Reagan administration, but the production schedule and limited resources dictated that CIA produce videos almost exclusively on subjects of interest to the President.

CONCLUSIONS

The view that Reagan was not a reader but at best a casual watcher of intelligence has been perpetuated by political conservatives and liberals, Democrats and Republicans alike. That view is not consistent with the general reappraisal of Reagan's intellectual abilities as evidenced by new scholarship over the past decade, but it has persisted. Logic and evidence, rather than political bias or personal opinion, paint a different picture. Logic would support the notion that Reagan, whom recent scholarship has established as an enthusiastic reader, was also a reader of intelligence, and new evidence presented herein has confirmed as myths the perceptions that Reagan was ignorant of intelligence, read little of it, and consumed it primarily in video form.

The record regarding Reagan's pre-presidential experiences as an actor, union leader, state governor, and especially as a member of the first high-level investigation of CIA (the Rockefeller Commission) indicates that these experiences gave the future president a background in and an understanding of many areas of intelligence, including espionage, secrecy, oversight and necessary safeguards, and the law. As a prolific radio commentator in the 1970s, Reagan reflected and propounded on intelligence issues of the day, particularly on the balance between democratic values and intelligence operations, the value of espionage and counterintelligence in the Cold War, and the damage to intelligence operations and CIA morale stemming from leaks, media exaggerations, and an overly intrusive Congress more interested in civil liberties than national security. The preponderance of direct and indirect evidence, beginning with detailed observations of Reagan's reading of the PDB as president-elect, conclusively demonstrates that he was an engaged and appreciative "First Customer" of intelligence who carefully read and used what he learned from intelligence products.

What are the lessons from this history for CIA officers? First, the conventional wisdom about presidents and intelligence may not be correct. Regarding any particular president's engagement with intelligence, it is better to rely more on observation than on hearsay. Second, during the transition period it may help to research the president-elect's background to determine what he or she actually understands about intelligence and how that person likes to receive information. This might help us to avoid surprises either pleasant—as in Reagan's case when he exceeded CIA's low expectations of him and the Agency learned that he was open to receiving a lot of intelligence material—or not so pleasant, if a future president-elect's background suggests an unfamiliarity or even hostility toward CIA's products (Richard Nixon comes to mind). Third, the true record gives us potential answers if we are asked by a future administration to deal with finished intelligence "like you did with Reagan." If CIA is ever asked, for example, to produce a daily intelligence video briefing like those provided for Reagan, the Agency—independent of its capability and will to do so at that time—can respond with "Actually, sir, that's a myth, and here are the data." Finally, it always is preferable to have the true picture about CIA's interactions with any president, for the Agency's influence, its missions, and the morale of its employees depend on that vital relationship.

APPENDIX

WILLIAM CASEY AND RONALD REAGAN: HOW CLOSE?

Because Casey is central to Ronald Reagan's war against the Soviet Union, understanding him and the part he played at CIA is critically important.

Robert Gates, *From the Shadows* (1996), p. 199.

Every organization—be it family, tribe, nation, or intelligence service—has its lore, its mythology, its memory of How Things Were and Came to Be. These received historical narratives can be problematic for the historian, who tries to understand and interpret for others the past as it was and on its own terms—not, for example, bringing a "present-mindedness" into historical inquiry that judges the past by the knowledge, standards or sensibilities of the present. Inevitably, however, the received narrative is often a mixture of the demonstrably true, the uncertain, the dubious, and the patently false—and the boundaries of all these categories constantly shift, thanks to the penchant of historians toward revisionism, re-revisionism, ad infinitum. Far from being fixed, the past is never over, it seems.

At CIA, there is an enduring internal narrative about the 1980s, specifically the years 1981 through 1986, when the Agency was led by Reagan's first DCI, William Casey. The "Reagan-Casey" years are understood as a time of resurgence for CIA, a second "Golden Age" for the Agency (the first was the Eisenhower-Dulles period, when CIA made a name for itself fighting the early Cold War). In the renewed and rejuvenated CIA of this narrative, CIA's relevance is reasserted after a difficult period for the Agency known as the Time of Troubles: the press revelations, scandals, and congressional investigations of the 1970s, combined with Jimmy Carter's perceived disdain for CIA as evidenced by the Carter administration's budget and personnel cuts under one of CIA's most disliked directors, Stansfield Turner. From an insider's perspective, the 1970s were a disaster. A CIA officer at the time with twenty years' service had joined in the Agency's heyday (during the first so-called Golden Age) but now saw an organization under siege.

Agency officers widely believe that William Casey gets the credit for resurrecting CIA with expanded resources and a renewed mission, thanks to his personal relationship, even intimate friendship, with the President. Casey, after all, had been Reagan's campaign manager, saving a bankrupt and dysfunctional primary campaign for "the Gipper" and overseeing the contest through to Reagan's electoral victory. Casey played up his closeness to Ronald Reagan, as expressed in this excerpt from an interview with Richard Lehman, a senior officer in the Directorate of Intelligence:

> Just after Christmas [1980] DCI-designate Bill Casey called Bruce [Clarke, the Deputy Director for Intelligence] and me in for a get-to-know-you session. We prepared the standard briefing, but

he interrupted us, saying in effect that he already understood all that. And he did. Apropos the relationship of the DCI to the President, he said, "You understand, I call him Ron."[53]

The phrase "I call him Ron"[54] summarizes the Agency's preferred thesis about this period—that CIA mattered in the 1980s largely because its director, William Casey, had a close friendship and an unprecedented influence with the President, manifested in his status as the first DCI with Cabinet rank, which Casey emphasized in his appearances before Agency employees.[55] It certainly was the impression of many senior CIA officials that, as one of them put it, "[Casey's] relationship with Ronald Reagan couldn't have been closer... It was clear to me that there was a very personal, a very close tie between those two men."[56] This perspective is reinforced by outside assessments; one historian of the period called Casey "perhaps the most influential man in the Reagan cabinet after the president."[57] The author of a CIA history highly regarded within the Agency said that Casey was "much more than just a director . . . he personally gave the CIA access to the president. In short, he was the most important thing about the agency."[58]

But was he? How valid is the perspective that Casey himself was the reason for CIA's renewed prominence during the Reagan years? Did Casey overstate his access to and intimacy with Ronald Reagan, or at least did he consciously fail to correct the impression at CIA that such a relationship existed? Casey's biographer Joseph Persico has documented that Casey early in his life freely embellished the level or degree of his access or influence. In 1940, for example, Casey, a young economic analyst and writer at the time, provided free market proposals to the presidential campaign of Thomas E. Dewey, a candidate for the Republican nomination, after which Casey claimed on his résumé that he had been a "tax and fiscal advisor" to Dewey. After Wendell Willkie defeated Dewey for the Republican nomination, Casey provided the same ideas to the Willkie campaign in the form of proposed language for speeches—becoming in his curriculum vitae a "Willkie speechwriter in the 1940 presidential campaign." While Persico's point is to portend the various controversies in Casey's later career—especially as DCI—that stemmed from Casey's arguably casual regard for the truth, it does seem more specifically that Casey was predisposed to overstate his relationship with Ronald Reagan.

That Casey did not have the relationship he touted is the assessment of Robert Gates, who was executive assistant to Casey in 1981-82, head of the Directorate of Intelligence (DI) in 1982-86, and then Casey's Deputy DCI. In a 1994 interview, Gates said

> I probably spent more time with Casey than anybody else in the Agency, and I just never had the sense that he had what I would call a close personal relationship

[with Reagan]. I think that his relationship with the president was in a considerable way a distant one.[59]

Gates explained this perspective more fully in his 1996 memoir:

I always believed that Bill Casey's closeness to Ronald Reagan was exaggerated. I think the relationship was closest in the first months of the administration, while there was still a genuine sense of gratitude on Reagan's part for Casey's management of the presidential campaign. . . Over time, however, their contacts grew less frequent. . . He could always get in to see the President when he wanted to, and could reach him on the phone, but he did so less and less as time passed.[60]

Preliminary research into DCI records confirms Gates's impression.[61] DCI daily schedules for calendar year 1981—the first eleven months of the first Reagan term—show that, while Casey as a Cabinet member saw President Reagan quite often at the White House as part of larger groups, he had surprisingly few personal meetings with Reagan. Starting with the first meeting of Reagan's NSC on 6 February 1981, through the end of December Casey attended at least 33 such meetings, 18 meetings of the National Security Policy Group (a subset of the NSC that dealt with policy toward the Soviet bloc and also intelligence activities), and 17 Cabinet meetings (often combined with a working lunch), for a total of 68 large-group White House meetings—an average of one every four days—not to mention an additional twelve White House social functions at which Casey and Reagan were both present. Casey may have sought to give the impression internally at CIA that many of his frequent trips to the White House were private visits with the President; Casey's schedule for 5 October, for example, lists "Lunch with the President," while Reagan's diary indicates it was lunch for 29 people.[62]

Casey's schedule for 1981, however, indicates he met alone with Reagan during this period only four times, or less than once every twelve weeks. In addition, he had six telephone conversations with the President. This is not the schedule of a man with a tremendously personal relationship with Ronald Reagan. Gates's impression that Casey's interactions with the President were most numerous in the first year (a view consistent with the fact that one of Casey's few close allies in the White House was Richard Allen, Reagan's national security advisor, who lasted just a year) is supported by a review of Casey's daily schedule for 1982. Casey in the second year of the Reagan administration saw the President in 54 large-group meetings (i.e. NSC, Cabinet, NSPG, down from 68 in 1981) and 5 small-group meetings; only three times did he meet with Reagan alone. Casey's telephone calls with the President in 1982 also dropped from the previous year, to four. The DCI's schedule for 1983 indicates he met privately with Reagan five times that year and had ten phone calls—up slightly from the preceding two years.[63] There is other evidence that in subsequent years Casey's individual meetings with Reagan and his telephone calls with him remained in low single digit figures.[64]

Curiously, especially because during the 1980 campaign Casey had believed that Reagan was capable of absorbing only a paragraph of text at one sitting, after the inauguration Casey began sending detailed and lengthy letters to the President on topics such as progress in rebuilding US intelligence capabilities, Soviet espionage, and arms talks and US-Soviet relations. These seem to have become longer and more frequent as time went on, perhaps to compensate for fewer personal meetings.[65]

Contrary to the conventional wisdom at CIA, it does not appear that the Agency's fortunes and influence during the Reagan administration rested entirely or even mostly on a close personal relationship between the DCI and the President. It is far more likely that CIA was influential because it served a President who understood intelligence and its importance, who appreciated how it would help him in policy decisions, and who appreciated the product CIA provided. These factors would have obtained for almost anyone Reagan chose to lead CIA. As it happened, he chose William Casey as a way to reward him for his crucial role in the campaign and because of his conservative views, particularly on foreign policy, that Reagan shared. History is not a science in that we can ever "run the experiment again," but it is fascinating to speculate that CIA might not have been worse off, and perhaps could have been better off, with someone other than Casey as DCI.

Note: The footnotes for this article are not included here for reasons of space. The full version, with footnotes, can be found on the DVD.

US INTELLIGENCE ESTIMATES OF THE SOVIET COLLAPSE:

REALITY AND PERCEPTION

Bruce D. Berkowitz

A commonly held belief is that the United States Intelligence Community (IC) failed to anticipate the collapse of the Soviet Union. Indeed, many of the U.S. officials who received intelligence about the Soviet Union, its decline in the late 1970s and 1980s, and its final crises in the 1989–1991 period, believe to this day that they were not warned——that they were, in effect, "blindsided."

This is odd, because the documented record shows that the Intelligence Community performed much better than most people seem to think. Indeed, this record suggests that U.S. intelligence provided about as good a product as one could reasonably expect. It detected the slowdown in the Soviet economy; it noted that the Soviet leadership was running out of options to save the country; it stipulated a set of conditions that might signal the crisis had reached a tipping point; and it notified top U.S. leaders when these conditions were met.

So these facts raise two questions: Why do so many people think the Intelligence Community failed? And why do many of the U.S. officials who were professional consumers of this intelligence still feel that they were not adequately warned? The nature of these questions should be noted before answers can be proffered.

In part, the questions are not about empirical realities, but about perceptions of those realities. To use a photography metaphor, the questions ask not about the "picture" out there, but about the "camera" in human heads. As such, the questions are not asking about the external conditions that produce surprise, but rather, the collective cognitive architecture of surprise. Put another way, leaders usually do not "get" blindsided; they blindside themselves by how they perceive intelligence, by the mental hurdles intelligence must surmount before it can change their perceptions, and in the constraints that limit their ability to act on information.

The questions are also about wishful thinking. Deep down, officials seem to want intelligence to make decisions for them, when, in reality, it rarely can.

THE RECORD, ON BACKGROUND

In 1995 Jeffrey T. Richelson brought to my attention several intelligence assessments and National Intelligence Estimates (NIEs) that had been declassified and cited in a study that Kirsten Lundberg carried out for the Kennedy School at Harvard.[1] Richelson, a scholar at the National Security Archive, is one of the most frequent users of the Freedom of Information Act (FOIA), and has over the years assembled an extensive database of declassified, leaked, and officially released intelligence products. When Richelson saw the citations in the Kennedy School study, he requested the documents under FOIA.

Richelson realized that these assessments were at odds with the popular conception that the Intelligence Community had failed to anticipate the collapse of the Soviet Union. The documents, since supplemented by others published by the CIA's Center for the Study of Intelligence, provide a factual basis for evaluating the IC's record. Richelson and I agreed to develop our own assessment of the U.S. Intelligence Community's performance, and to consider how the distorted views of its Soviet analyses had developed. We interviewed most of the officials who participated in developing the analysis and several of the key consumers who served in the White House under President George H. W. Bush.[2]

We concluded that the performance of the U.S. Intelligence Community in anticipating the decline and collapse of the Soviet Union was generally good and sometimes outstanding. The Intelligence Community faced three basic tasks:

- First, analysts had to detect the overall slowdown of the Soviet economy and assess the underlying political, economic, and demographic factors that would make it difficult, if not impossible, for the Soviets to recover. This long-range analytical task had a time frame of approximately five to ten years, partly because that is the length of time such tidal socioeconomic changes require, and also because that encompasses several U.S. electoral cycles. This long-range warning gives elected officials time to reshape U.S. strategy and the electorate time to absorb and (perhaps) support it.

- Second, the Intelligence Community had to detect shorter-range trends that could plausibly lead to a crisis in Soviet politics and trigger collapse. Analysts had to postulate plausible scenarios and, as the Soviet Union drew closer to a crisis state, compare the probability of one scenario with another. This kind of warning, with a one-to-five-year time frame, permits a President to make significant adjustments during his term. The challenge here was partly one of imagination, and partly one of understanding how to weigh the various political and economic factors that would determine the outcome.

- Third, the IC had to warn U.S. officials when the Soviet collapse was imminent and the final endgame under way. The time frame for this task was a year or less. Analysts had to postulate specific "gates" that developments would need to pass through for the endgame to be triggered and then determine whether those gates had been passed.

Each task required an increasing level of specificity and, by extension, that there were three opportunities in which U.S. intelligence analysts could fail. These levels of warning are also interrelated. If analysts and officials are unaware of strategic changes in their adversary, they are less likely to succeed at tactical warning, and if they have failed the tactical problem, they will more likely be unprepared for the task of immediate warning.

LONG-RANGE WARNING

The challenge of anticipating the Soviet collapse was even greater for U.S. intelligence because the very notion of collapse was inconsistent with the thinking of most Western analysts and scholars. The prevailing view up to the late 1970s was that the Soviet Union would evolve, not collapse. True, some Sovietologists had long believed that a multiethnic, nondemocratic state dependent on a centrally planned economy was inherently unstable. Indeed, that was the assumption upon which containment was based.[3] But hardly any of these scholars were willing to hazard a time frame for a Soviet implosion. So their views were more of a theory than an intelligence estimate.

But by the mid-1970s there were growing signs that the Soviet economy and political system had ingrained, systemic problems. In the Intelligence Community, this economic slowdown was a basic underlying assumption for most intelligence analyses of the Soviet Union from the mid-1970s onward. Up to then, assessments often cited problems in the Soviet economy such as agricultural shortfalls and competition for resources and manufacturing capacity. After this point, the general understanding was that the Soviet Union as a whole was stagnating or declining economically, and that this slowdown would have profound political effects.

The main disagreement within the Intelligence Community was about how severe the effects of economic stagnation might be and how the Soviets would deal with them. The CIA and the Defense Intelligence Agency (DIA) took different approaches to measuring gross domestic product. In addition, while the CIA believed the economic slowdown might hinder the Soviet military buildup, the DIA believed that the continuing evidence of a military buildup illustrated that the Soviets were determined to outpace the United States despite economic constraints.

But hardly anyone in the IC—especially the CIA—argued that the Soviets were in great shape, despite what some critics of the Agency might suggest today. For example, in July 1977, the CIA reported the following:

> The Soviet economy faces serious strains in the decade ahead. The simple growth formula upon which the economy has relied for more than a generation—maximum inputs of labor and capital—will no longer yield the sizeable annual growth which has provided resources needed for competing claims. . . . Reduced growth, as is foreshadowed over the next decade, will make pursuit of these objectives much more difficult, and pose hard choices for the leadership, which can have a major impact on Soviet relations with Eastern Europe and the West.[4]

This assessment of a stagnating Soviet economy was, in turn, reflected in U.S. national strategy. Presidential Directive 18, which defined U.S. national strategy in the Carter administration, said that, "though successfully acquiring military power matching the United States, the Soviet Union continues to face major internal economic and national difficulties, and externally it has few genuinely committed allies while lately suffering setbacks in its relations with China, parts of Africa, and India."[5]

The Reagan administration went a step further by arguing that the United States could take advantage of these weaknesses and, through a planned, integrated strategy, accelerate the metamorphosis of the Communist regime. The resulting policy was a combination of economic pressure (through an arms race and trade sanctions) and political and military pressure (by supporting opponents of the Soviets and their allies in Eastern Europe, Latin America, and especially Afghanistan). According to National Security Decision Directive 32, U.S. goals were to "foster, if possible in concert with our allies, restraint in Soviet military spending, discourage Soviet adventurism, and weaken the Soviet alliance system by forcing the USSR to bear the brunt of its economic shortcomings, and to encourage long-term liberalizing and nationalist tendencies within the Soviet Union and allied countries."[6]

In the late 1970s, though, before he became President, not even Ronald Reagan was willing to propose that the Soviet Union was on a course to collapse. In his speeches and essays during this period, Reagan was fully prepared to argue that the Soviet Union was evil, and that its economy was inefficient and unable to sustain itself indefinitely. But he was not ready to say that it was on a course to collapse or that U.S. policy could accelerate this collapse. Reagan did not make those statements until after he entered office, specifically in his June 1982 address to the British Parliament, and his March 1983 speech to the National Association of Evangelicals.[7]

If the documentary record is clear, then why do so many people believe that the Intelligence Community failed to detect the Soviet Union's social and economic problems in the late 1970s?

One reason may have been that, at the time, the Soviet Union seemed ascendant. It had matched and even surpassed the United States in several measures of military capability, such as numbers of intercontinental ballistic missiles. It had expanded its influence through military cooperation treaties with clients in Asia, Africa, and the Middle East. The popular media (and the Intelligence Community) duly reported these events, and so the zeitgeist was that the Soviets were strong, and the United States was stuck in malaise. Since American officials did not effectively challenge this view in public, Americans logically concluded later that this reflected the intelligence they were reading.

Besides, nothing was inevitable about a Soviet collapse in the late 1970s. At that point, many outcomes were possible. A more ruthless leader might have held the state together for another ten or fifteen years; witness Alexander Lukashenko in Belarus and Kim Jong-Il in North Korea. A more flexible leader might have managed a "soft landing" for the Soviet Communist Party; witness the current situation in China. To provide a more definitive estimate fifteen years before the fact was impossible because the future was not yet certain. It never is.

INTERMEDIATE AND IMMEDIATE WARNING

By the early 1980s, the faltering Soviet economy was a given, the assumed context within which the Intelligence Community viewed Soviet political and military developments. For example, in 1985, as Mikhail Gorbachev took control, the National Intelligence Estimate on the Soviet domestic scene encapsulated the fundamental weaknesses in the Soviet state. It did not yet say that the conditions for collapse were present, but it explained how such a path was possible:

The growth of the Soviet economy has been systematically decelerating since the 1950s as a consequence of dwindling supplies of new labor, the increasing cost of raw material inputs, and the constraints on factor productivity improvement imposed by the rigidities of the planning and management system. . . .

The USSR is afflicted with a complex of domestic maladies that seriously worsened in the late 1970s and early 1980s. Their alleviation is one of the most significant and difficult challenges facing the Gorbachev regime. . . .

Over the next five years, and for the foreseeable future, the troubles of the society will not present a challenge to the system of political control that guarantees Kremlin rule, nor will they threaten the economy with collapse. But, during the rest of the 1980s and well beyond, the domestic affairs of the USSR will be dominated by the efforts of the regime to grapple with these manifold problems. . . .

Gorbachev has achieved an upswing in the mood of the Soviet elite and populace. But the prospects for his strategy over the next five years are mixed at best. . . .[8]

It is noteworthy that the forecasting horizon of the 1985 NIE was five years—normal for an NIE—and that the Soviet collapse occurred just beyond that horizon. But it was still premature in 1985 for a definitive forecast. As the Soviet situation got progressively worse, so did the prognosis by the Intelligence Community. By spring 1989—more than two years before the attempted coup that led to the ultimate collapse of the regime—the IC was telling U.S. leaders that the situation was essentially irretrievable and that a catastrophic end (from the Soviet leadership's point of view) was possible. The 1989 NIE said: "It will be very difficult for [Gorbachev] to achieve his goals. In the extreme, his policies and political power could be undermined and the political stability of the Soviet system could be fundamentally threatened. . . . [A]nxiety, fear, and anger [of the Soviet political elite] could still crystallize in an attempted coup, legal removal of Gorbachev, or even assassination."[9]

In April 1991 the Office of Soviet Analysis (SOVA), the office within the Directorate of Intelligence that followed developments in the USSR, told U.S. leaders explicitly that the Soviet Union was in a state of crisis, offered a poor prognosis, and spelled out specific scenarios in which the regime could implode. In a memo titled, "The Soviet Cauldron," SOVA's director wrote,

> The economy is in a downward spiral with no end in sight . . . inflation was about 20 percent at the end of last year and will be at least double that this year . . . reliance on a top-down approach to problems, particularly in regard to republics, has generated a war of laws between various levels of power and created a legal mess to match the economic mess. . . . In this situation of growing chaos, explosive events have become increasingly possible.[10]

The memo then went on to describe possible outcomes, which included the assassination of Gorbachev or Boris Yeltsin, or a coup by "reactionary leaders who judge that the last chance to act had come"—which is, of course, exactly what later occurred.

Did the Intelligence Community provide immediate warning of the coup that triggered the final events of 1991? George W. H. Bush recalls in his memoirs:

> Besides the coup rumors in July, which Gorbachev had dismissed, there had been some recent indication that the hard-liners in Moscow might be up to something. On Saturday morning, August 17, Bob Gates had joined me at breakfast where we went over the Presidential Daily Briefing. In it was a report that the prospective signing of the Union treaty meant that time was running out for the hard-liners and they might feel compelled to act. Bob thought the threat was serious, although we had no specific information on what might happen or when. The next day the plotters struck.[11]

Robert M. Gates, then deputy national security advisor, and soon to become Director of Central Intelligence (DCI), and currently Secretary of Defense, recalled the same briefing this way:

> CIA warned us at the White House that once the signing date [for the Union treaty] was set a deadline of sorts would be established for the conservatives to act. The changes that would follow signature, together with public sentiment, would make action after that date much more difficult. . . . [I]t fell to me on August 17 to hand the President his CIA President's Daily Brief,

which warned of the strong chance that the conservatives would act within the next few days. It said, "The danger is growing that hardliners will precipitate large-scale violence" and described their efforts to prepare for an attempt to seize power. . . . [Bush] asked me if I thought the situation was serious and if the Agency's warning was valid. I explained the meaning of the August 20 signing ceremony, and said I thought he should take the PDB warning quite seriously.[12]

Note how Bush and Gates score this event differently, even though they basically agree on the facts. Gates believes he gave Bush warning because the CIA had previously established the prerequisite conditions for there to be a coup, and he says that the President's daily briefing for 17 August indicated that those conditions were present. Bush wanted to know whether any specific datum indicated what might happen or when, but Gates had no such specific datum.

These two different slants on the same material suggest just how controversial an assessment of whether one was "blindsided" can be, and they also highlight exactly where, if anywhere, the Intelligence Community fell short. To reach this last step in anticipating the Soviet collapse, the CIA would have needed first-hand information from the plotters themselves. Analysis alone can never fill that kind of gap, if only because an analysis is at best a probability assessment necessarily based on inference and deduction. The key datum that was lacking was, as Bush put it, the "specific information on what might happen or when." This was a very tough piece of information to collect. Even Gorbachev lacked it, obviously.

THE PERSISTENT MYTH—WHY?

All in all, this is a good record. So why has the Intelligence Community's performance been so underappreciated, and why do officials to this day believe they were poorly served? What collective cognitive architecture explains the gap between the record and the perceptions, then and ever since?

One key reason is that the written record remained classified for several years after the Soviet Union disintegrated. Even when the most important documents, the National Intelligence Estimates, were declassified, they were initially not made widely available. Without being able to point to specific documents that presented the Intelligence Community's consensus, the idea that the IC was caught flat-footed took root by default.

One example shows how such an information vacuum can be perpetuated into a "truth" with major effects. In 1991, former Director of Central Intelligence Stansfield Turner published an article on the general topic of the future of intelligence. In one passage, Turner cited the apparent failure of the Intelligence Community to anticipate the Soviet collapse:

> We should not gloss over the enormity of this failure to forecast the magnitude of the Soviet crisis. We know now that there were many Soviet academics, economists and political thinkers, other than those officially presented to us by the Soviet government, who understood long before 1980 that the Soviet economic system was broken and that it was only a matter of time before someone had to try to repair it, as had Khrushchev. Yet I never heard a suggestion from the CIA, or the intelligence arms of the departments of defense or state, that numerous Soviets recognized a growing, systemic economic problem. . . . Today we hear some revisionist rumblings that the CIA did in fact see the Soviet collapse emerging after all. If some individual CIA analysts were more prescient than the corporate view, their ideas were filtered out in the bureaucratic process; and it is the corporate view that counts because that is what reaches the president and his advisers. On this one, the corporate view missed by a mile. . . . Why were so many of us so insensitive to the inevitable?[13]

This quotation has been repeated many times. It is usually portrayed as a mea culpa from a former head of the U.S. Intelligence Community, seemingly acknowledging that the community had failed to anticipate the Soviet collapse. However, it requires some parsing.

When Turner said he "never heard a suggestion" of a systemic weakness of the Soviet system, he was referring to the period he served as DCI, 1977– 1981. Also, when he criticized "revisionist rumblings" claiming the CIA did anticipate the collapse, neither the intelligence assessments reporting the Soviet decline in the 1980s nor the policy directives they supported had yet been released.

In reality, both the opinion of "individual CIA analysts," such as the director of SOVA, and the "corporate view" expressed in NIEs, concluded that the Soviet Union was in decline throughout the 1980s. These views were reaching the President and, as indicated earlier, were incorporated into presidential directives. But this paper trail was not made public until four years after Turner wrote. Indeed, the inherent problems and the decline of the Soviet economy had become the working assumption on which U.S. intelligence was based by the time Turner left office.

Nevertheless, this single quotation by Turner was cited repeatedly and written into the public record. Most notably, the late Senator Daniel Patrick Moynihan (D, NY) referred to it during the confirmation hearing of Robert Gates to be Director of Central Intelligence in 1991; included it in the 1996 report of the Commission on Protecting and Reducing Government Secrecy, which he chaired; cited it in Secrecy: The American Experience, a book he published in 1988; repeated it in an interview on The NewsHour with Jim Lehrer in 1998; mentioned it in his farewell speech to the U.S. Senate in 2002; and quoted it in his commencement address at Harvard in 2003. During this entire period, however, one is unable to find a single instance in which Moynihan quotes from an actual intelligence publication, such as those declassified in the early 1990s. Even when Moynihan submitted a bill in 1995 to abolish the CIA, he introduced the bill with a speech on the Senate floor that again claimed the Intelligence Community had failed to anticipate the Soviet collapse—and that again offered as its only evidence the aforementioned Turner quotation.[14] Despite its paucity of actual evidence, the impact of Moynihan's proposal was significant. It was (along with reaction to the Aldrich Ames espionage affair and concerns over the performance of intelligence in the First Gulf War) responsible for the establishment of the Aspin-Brown Commission and the contentious intelligence reforms of 1996.[15]

Squaring the documented record with Turner's comment from 1991 is difficult. Perhaps Turner simply was unaware of the mainstream opinion of the Intelligence Community in the 1980s, after he left office. Even more difficult is the reconciliation of the views of anyone who did have access to intelligence and still believes that the CIA and other agencies failed to provide warning. But this is precisely what the phenomenon of being blindsided is all about. The perception of being warned becomes separated from the reality of the warning that was provided. The best to be said is that this may be a problem more appropriately examined in the discipline of psychology, rather than in history or political science.

Those who criticize the IC's assessment of the Soviet Union often get caught up in details, faulting it on specific findings that were secondary to the larger picture it was painting. In the early 1980s, the CIA believed the Soviet gross domestic product was growing at about two percent annually. Today we know that its economic growth was essentially nonexistent. But the CIA was not trying to make the case that the Soviet Union was growing; as indicated, the two percent growth estimate reflected a conclusion that, after remarkable growth in the 1950s and 1960s, the Soviet economy was grinding to a halt. The growth estimates were based on a modeling process that was controversial even at the time, and should not divert attention from the key judgments that summarized the Intelligence Community's bedrock views—that the Soviet Union was in trouble.

WHY DO OFFICIALS FEEL ILL-SERVED?

One interesting feature about the controversies over the Soviet collapse is that some officials who had read the intelligence and understood full well what it said still believe they were, in some important sense, surprised when the end came. When Gorbachev was toppled, it seemed as though the Bush 41 administration was not prepared to respond. Some critics wondered why Bush had not moved earlier to embrace Yeltsin, who ultimately prevailed. Would better intelligence have made a difference?

The first President Bush described the warning presented to him as too limited for taking action. But his diary entry on 19 August 1991 suggests that more factors were in play than just this intelligence report. Reflecting on the day's events, Bush wrote:

> [T]he questions for the most part were okay; [such as] "Why were you surprised?" There will be a lot of talking heads analyzing the policy, but in my view this totally vindicates our policy of trying to stay with Gorbachev. If we had pulled the rug out from under Gorbachev and swung toward Yeltsin you'd have seen a military crackdown far in excess of the ugliness that's taking place now. I'm convinced of that. I think what we must do is see that the progress made under Gorbachev is not turned around.[16]

In other words, the Bush administration—despite receiving and acknowledging that conditions were ripe for a coup—believed it had no option other than to stick with Gorbachev. This was a judgment based less on intelligence information or the lack thereof than on the administration's policy objectives. The administration's goals were established by National Security Directive 23, which Bush signed on 22 September 1989:

> Our policy is not designed to help a particular leader or set of leaders in the Soviet Union. We seek, instead, fundamental alterations in Soviet military force structure, institutions, and practices which can only be reversed at great cost, economically and politically, to the Soviet Union. If we succeed, the ground for cooperation will widen, while that for conflict narrows. The U.S.–Soviet relationship may still be fundamentally competitive, but it will be less militarized and safer. . . . U.S. policy will encourage fundamental political and economic reform, including freely contested elections, in East-Central Europe, so that states in that region may once again be productive members of a prosperous, peaceful, and democratic Europe, whole and free of fear of Soviet intervention.[17]

In short, the Bush administration did not intend to destabilize the Soviet Union (though it did envision the breakup of the Warsaw Pact). This is a subtle, but significant, difference from the policy of the Reagan administration, which said that the United States would seek to exploit fissures within the Warsaw Pact and the weakness of the Soviet economy. The Bush administration, in contrast, aimed to use economic pressure as a means to encourage the existing regime to moderate. National Security Directive 23 said:

> The purpose of our forces is not to put pressure on a weak Soviet economy or to seek military superiority. Rather, U.S. policy recognizes the need to provide a hedge against uncertain long-term developments in the Soviet Union and to impress upon the Soviet leadership the wisdom of pursuing a responsible course. . . . Where possible, the United States should promote Western values and ideas within the Soviet Union, not in the spirit of provocation or destabilization, but as a means to lay a firm foundation for a cooperative relationship.

Note that the directive says "impress upon the Soviet leadership [emphasis added]"—meaning that the U.S. leadership expected the Soviet regime to remain in place as the directive was implemented. The Reagan administration's view was different, as expressed in President Reagan's address to the British Parliament on 8 June 1982:

> I have discussed on other occasions . . . the elements of Western policies toward the Soviet Union to safeguard our interests and protect the peace. What I am describing now is a plan and a hope for the long term——the march of freedom and democracy which will leave Marxism-Leninism on the ash-heap of history as it has left other tyrannies which stifle the freedom and muzzle the self-expression of the people.[18]

In other words, the Reagan administration might not have sought the collapse of the Soviet regime, but it envisioned that the regime would fall, and thus would have been less surprised by the collapse. Significantly, the Reagan policy was adopted before Gorbachev rose to power and provided, in the words of Great Britain's then–Prime Minister, Margaret Thatcher, someone with whom "we can do business." Had there been a third Reagan administration, it might have come to resemble the Bush administration as it adjusted to changes in Soviet realities.

In any event, the Bush policy was predicated on continuing to deal with the Soviet regime. So when the regime collapsed, as Bush recalled, the natural tendency was for observers to ask if the administration had been caught unaware. Apparently it was, but if so, that was not because of an intelligence failure, but rather the result of an intentional policy decision to support Gorbachev to the end.

THE REAL THING

Americans know what an actual intelligence failure looks like. Recall, for example, the August 1978 assessment by the CIA that "Iran is not in a revolutionary or even a pre-revolutionary state," six months before the Shah fell.[19] Or more recently, the October 2002 NIE, which said that, "in the view of most agencies, Baghdad is reconstituting its nuclear weapons program."[20] Analysts lose sleep over these kinds of statements because, despite the cliche´ about coordinated intelligence reflecting the lowest common denominator, a hallmark of American intelligence analysis is the constant pressure to publish clear, definitive statements. So when the analysis is wrong, it is apt to be clearly wrong.

Conversely, when it is correct, it is clearly correct. Only the most convoluted reasoning can turn the summaries and key judgments of the Intelligence Community's analysis of the Soviet Union in the 1980s into a case that the IC "missed" the Soviet collapse.

Holding intelligence organizations accountable for their performance is important. But acknowledging when intelligence is successful is equally important. So, too, is appreciating the differences between an intelligence failure and policy frailties whose sources lie elsewhere. Without an understanding that such things can happen, being blindsided in the future is certain.

Note: The footnotes for this article are not included here for reasons of space. The full version, with footnotes, can be found on the DVD.

WHAT SHOULD WE EXPECT OF INTELLIGENCE?

Gregory F. Treverton

When I ran the process that produced America's National Intelligence Estimates (NIEs), I took comfort when I was told that predictions of continuity beat any weather forecaster– if it was fine, predict fine weather until it rained, then predict rain until it turned fine. I mused, if those forecasters, replete with data, theory and history, can't predict the weather, how can they expect us to predict a complicated human event like the collapse of the Soviet Union? The question behind the musing was what should people expect of their intelligence agencies? Not what they'd like, for policymakers would like perfect prescience if not omniscience, though they know they can have neither.

THE POWER OF "STORY"

Reasonably, expectations should differ across different intelligence problems. But start with that hoary Soviet case: should intelligence services have done better in foreseeing the end of the Soviet Union? After all, the premise of the West's containment strategy was that if Soviet expansion were contained, eventually the empire would collapse from its own internal contradictions. So some monitoring of how that policy was doing would have seemed appropriate.

In retrospect, there were signs aplenty of a sick society. Emigrés arrived with tales of Soviet toasters that were as likely to catch fire as to brown bread. The legendary demographer, Murray Feshbach, came back to Washington in the mid-1970s with a raft of Soviet demographics, most of which, like male life expectancy, were going in the wrong direction for a rich country. These factoids were puzzling, but we rationalized the first on the grounds that the Soviet defense industry was special and apart from ordinary Soviet industry; the second we dismissed with "Russians drink too much" or some such. Emmanuel Todd did Feshbach one better and turned the demographic numbers into a prediction of the Soviet Union's collapse. But he suffered the double misfortune of not only being, but also writing in French, and so was not likely to make much of a dent in official Washington.

Intelligence is about creating and adjusting stories – or so it has come to seem to me in a career as a producer and consumer of intelligence – and in the 1970s and into the 1980s, the story in the heads of policymakers was Soviet expansion abroad, not disintegration at home. Thus, those Feshbach statistics were just curious factoids. The Soviet invasion of Afghanistan, the Evil Empire and "star wars" were still in the future. Imagine an intelligence officer who had tried to explain to the newly elected Ronald Reagan that the Soviet problem he faced was not power but impending collapse. That analyst would soon have found himself counting Soviet submarines in the Aleutian Islands. Questions not asked or stories not imagined by policy are not likely to be answered or developed by intelligence.

The best point prediction of Soviet implosion I have seen was a slightly whimsical piece written by the British columnist, Bernard Levin, in September 1977. He got the process exactly right: change would come not from the bottom but from the top, from Soviet leaders who "are in every respect model Soviet functionaries. Or rather, in every respect but one: they have admitted the truth about their country to themselves, and have vowed, also to themselves, to do something about it." Levin didn't get the motivation of the high-level revolutionaries right – he imagined a deep-seated lust for freedom, rather than concern over the stagnating Soviet economy – but at least he had a story. For the sake of convenience, he picked the 200th anniversary of the French revolution as the date – July 14, 1989.

Closer to the end, CIA assessments were on the mark but still lacked for a story. The Agency had been pointing to a chronic slowdown in the Soviet economy since the 1970s, and a 1981 report was blunt: "The Soviet pattern in many respects conforms to that of a less developed country. There is remarkably little progress toward a more modern pattern." By 1982, CIA assessments concluded that Soviet defense spending had stopped growing, and the next year revised their previous assessments, concluding that defense spending had tailed off beginning in 1976.

Interestingly, those who could imagine the story didn't believe it could be true. Unlike Levin, they did not believe the Soviet Union could be reformed from the top. And in that they turned out to be right. The director of America's eavesdroppers, the National Security Agency, Lt. Gen. William Odom wrote in 1987 that the Mikhail Gorbachev's program, if followed to its logical conclusion, would lead to Gorbachev's political suicide and the collapse of the system. Because this did not seem what Gorbachev had in mind, he and others, including Robert Gates, then the Deputy Director of Central Intelligence, concluded that Gorbachev could not intend to do what he said he would.

In fact, the Soviet Union didn't have to end in 1991. Indeed, it might still be doddering along today but for the actions of that visionary bumbler, Mikhail Gorbachev, who understood his nation's weakness but had no idea how to deal with it, and so set in motion an economic reform program that was pain for not much gain. What we could have expected of intelligence is not prediction but earlier and better monitoring of internal shortcomings. We could also have expected some imaginings of competing stories to the then prevailing one. Very late, in 1990, an NIE, The Deepening Crisis in the USSR, did just that, laying out four different scenarios, or stories, for the next year.

PUZZLES AND MYSTERIES

When the Soviet Union would collapse was a mystery, not a puzzle. No one could know the answer. It depended. It was contingent. Puzzles are a very different kind of intelligence problem. They have an answer, but we may not know it. Many of the intelligence successes of the Cold War were puzzle-solving about a very secretive foe: Were there Soviet missiles in Cuba? How many warheads did the Soviet SS-18 missile carry?

Puzzles are not necessarily easier than mysteries – consider the decade it took to finally solve the puzzle of Osama bin Laden's whereabouts. But they do come with different expectations attached. Intelligence puzzles are not like jig-saw puzzles in that we may not be very sure we have the right answer – the raid on bin Laden was launched, participants in the decision said, with odds that bin Laden actually was in the compound no better than six in ten. But the fact that there is in principle an answer provides some concreteness to what is expected of intelligence.

That is especially so at the more tactical level of intelligence. In the simplest case, targeting (or producing, in wonderful Pentagonese, "desired mean points of impact," DMPIs, pronounced "dimpies"), the enemy unit either is or isn't where intelligence says it is. And the intelligence will quickly be self-validating as the fighter pilot or drone targeter discovers whether the enemy unit is in fact there. The raid on bin Laden's compound reflected the solution to a much more complicated puzzle, one that was a nice example of the various forms of collection and analysis working together. But in that case too it would have been immediately apparent to the raiders if bin Laden hadn't been there.

Another puzzle, whether Saddam Hussein's Iraq had weapons of mass destruction (WMD) in 2002, drives home the point that because intelligence is a service industry, what policy officials expect from it shapes its work. In the WMD case, neither the U.S. investigating panel nor the British Butler report found evidence that political leaders had directly pressured intelligence agencies to come to a particular conclusion. Yet it is also fair to report that some intelligence analysts on both sides of the Atlantic did feel they were under pressure to produce the "right" answer – that Saddam Hussein had weapons of mass destruction.

The interaction of intelligence and policy shaped the results in several other ways. Policy officials, particularly on the American side, when presented with a range of assessments by different agencies, cherry picked their favorites (and sometimes grew their own cherries by giving credibility to information sources the intelligence services had discredited). As elsewhere in life, how the question was asked went a long way toward determining the answer. In this case, the question became simply "Does Saddam have WMD?" Intelligence analysis did broaden the question, but issues of how much threat, to whom and over what time frame got lost in the "does he?" debate. Moreover, U.S. intelligence was asked over and over about links between Iraq and al Qaeda. It stuck to its analytic guns – the link was tenuous at best – but the repeated questions served both to elevate the debate over the issue and to contribute to intelligence's relative lack of attention to other questions.

In the end, however, the most significant part of the WMD story was what intelligence and policy shared – a deeply held mindset that Saddam must have WMD. That mindset included outsiders like me who opposed going to war, as well as other European intelligence services whose governments were not going to participate in any war. For intelligence, the mindset was compounded by history, for the previous time around, in the early 1990s, U.S. intelligence had underestimated Iraqi WMD; it was not going to make that mistake again. In the end, if most people believe one thing, arguing for another is hard. There is little pressure to rethink the issue, and the few dissenters in intelligence are lost in the wilderness.

What should have been expected from intelligence in this case was a section in the assessments asking what was the best case that could be made that Iraq did not have WMD. That would not have made the slightest bit of difference in the rush to war, given the power of the prevailing mindset, but it would at least offered intelligence agencies some protection from later criticism – fair enough – that they had not done their job.

What policy officials expect from intelligence also shapes how intelligence is organized and what kind of people it hires. On the American side of the Atlantic, the crown jewel of intelligence products is the President's Daily Brief (PDB), perhaps the most expensive publication per copy since Gutenberg. Often caricatured as "CNN plus secrets," much of it is factoids from recent collection by a spy or satellite image or intercepted signal, plus commentary. On the British side of the ocean, there is less of a flood of current intelligence, and the assessments of the UK's Joint Intelligence Committee are, in my experience, often thoughtful. But on both sides of the ocean, the tyranny of the immediate is apparent. As one U.S. analyst put it to me: "We used to do analysis; now we do reporting."

The focus on the immediate, combined with the way intelligence agencies are organized, may have played some role in the failure to understand the contagion effects in the "Arab spring" of recent months. In the United States, especially, where analytic cadres are large, analysts have very specific assignments. The Egypt analysts are tightly focused on Egypt, perhaps even on particular aspects of Egypt. They would not been looking at ways events in Tunisia might affect Egypt. To be fair, the popular media probably overstated the contagion effect of events from one Arab country to the next, but that there was some such effect seems apparent in retrospect. Worse, my bet is that if asked whether events in Tunisia might affect Egypt, even slightly, those Egypt analysts would have said "no" with more or less disdain.

In the end, what is expected of intelligence also shapes what capabilities it builds – and hires. At the tactical level, teams of young analysts from the big U.S. collection agencies (the National Security Agency for signals intelligence or SIGINT and the National Geospatial Intelligence Agency for imagery, or IMINT), organized into "geocells" have become adept at combining SIGINT and imagery, and adding what has been learned from informants in the battle zones, in order to identify events of interests, and ultimately provide those DIMPIs.

The demand for those DIMPIs is plain enough, and the PDB's unusually collected secrets are beguiling if not always very helpful. The demand from policy officials for more strategic, and perhaps longer-term, assessments is less clear. When asked, officials say they would like them: how could they answer otherwise? But in practice too often the response is: "That looks interesting. I'll read it when there is time." And there never is time. When I was at the National Intelligence Council (NIC) overseeing NIEs we had a good idea. We'd do a short intelligence appraisal of an important foreign policy issue, and the State Department's policy planners would add a policy paper. We'd then convene the deputies – the number twos in the various foreign policy agencies – over an informal lunch. The conversation would begin with the outcome the United States sought a decade out, then peel back to current policy. We got such a session on the deputies' calendar exactly once.

Lacking demand, it is not at all clear that intelligence agencies either hire or train people who could do good strategic analysis – that is, analysis that locates choices in a wider context of other issues and perhaps a longer time stream. Most analysts are trained to look for measurable evidence and struggle with alternative possibilities, but are not always willing to venture beyond the facts and the level of policy description. To be sure, there are differences across agencies. The State Department's Bureau of Intelligence and Research, while small, does value deep expertise, letting analysts stay on a particular account for an entire career. By contrast, the analytic arm of the CIA believes good analysts can add value quickly as they move from account to account. As a result, it has more the feel of a newsroom than a university.

At the NIC, I came to think that, for all the technology, strategic analysis was best done in person. Indeed, I came to think that our real products weren't those papers, the NIEs. Rather they were the NIOs, the National Intelligence Officers – experts not papers. We all think we can absorb information more efficiently by reading, but my advice to my policy colleagues was to give intelligence officers some face time. If policymakers ask for a paper, what they get inevitably will be 60 degrees off the target. In 20 minutes, though, the intelligence officers can sharpen the question, and the policy official can calibrate the expertise of the analyst. In that conversation, intelligence analysts can offer advice; they don't need to be as tightly restricted as on paper by the "thou shalt not traffic in policy" injunction. Expectations can be calibrated on both sides of the conversation. And the result might even be better policy.

Note: The footnotes for this article are not included here for reasons of space. The full version, with footnotes, can be found on the DVD.

THE REAGAN COLD WAR TIMELINE
1981 - 1989

9 FEB
Yuri Andropov dies after only 15 months as Soviet leader.

13 FEB
Konstantin Chernenko, at age 72, is named General Secretary of the Soviet Communist Party.

20 JAN
Ronald Reagan inaugurated 40th President of the United States.

10 NOV
Soviet General Secretary Leonid Brezhnev dies.

24 MAY
President Reagan visits CIA HQs for the groundbreaking on the new headquarters building.

8 MAR
In a speech to the National Association of Evangelicals, Reagan labels the Soviet Union an "evil empire."

16 DEC
Margaret Thatcher and the UK Government, in a plan to open new channels of dialog with the Soviet leadership candidates, meet with Mikhail Gorbachev at Chequers.

1981	1982	1983	1984	1985

1 SEP
Civilian Koran Air Lines Flight 007, with 269 passengers, is shot down by Soviet interceptor aircraft.

16 MAR
Chernenko, after just more thana year in office, dies in Moscow. Search for new leader begins.

23 MAR
Ronald Reagan proposes the Strategic Defense Initiative (SDI, or Star Wars).

11 MAR
Mikhail Gorbachev becomes new leader of the USSR. He was the only general secretary in the history of the Soviet Union to be born under Communist rule.

12 NOV
Yuri Andropov becomes General Secretary of the Soviet Union.

23 JUN
President Reagan visits CIA HQs to sign the Intelligence Identities Protection Act.

19-20 NOV
Reagan and Gorbachev meet
for the first time at a summit in
Geneva, Switzerland, where they
agree to two (later three) more
summits.

11-12 OCT
Reykjavik Summit: a breakthrough
in nuclear arms control, but SDI
remains a sticking point.

9 NOV
The Berlin Wall is breached
when a Politburo spokesman
mistakenly announces at a news
conference in East Berlin that
the borders have been opened.

26 MAY
President Reagan visits CIA
HQs for the swearing in ceremony
of William Webster as DCI.

8 DEC ∎
The Intermediate-Range Nuclear
Forces (INF) Treaty is signed in
Washington, DC by President Reagan
and Soviet leader Gorbachev.

15 MAY
The Soviets begin with-
drawing from Afghanistan.

1986   1987   1988   1989   1990

26 APR
Chernobyl disaster: A Soviet
nuclear plant in Ukraine
explodes, resulting in the worst
nuclear power plant accident
in history.

JUN
At the June plenary session of
the Central Committee of the
Communist Party, Gorbachev
announces Glasnost and
Perestroyka, which laid
the political foundation
of economic reform for the
remainder of the existence
of the Soviet Union

29 MAY
Reagan and Gorbachev meet
in Moscow. INF Treaty ratified.
When asked if he still believes
that the Soviet Union is an evil
empire, Reagan replies he was
talking about "another time,
another place."

12 JUN
During a visit to Berlin,
Germany, President Reagan
famously challenges Soviet
leader Gorbachev in a speech
to "tear down this wall"
(the Berlin Wall).

Intelligence

Dimensions of Civil Unrest
in the Soviet Union

National Intelligence Council
Memorandum

This Memorandum has been coordinated within
the National Intelligence Council and with the
Directorate of Operations. It has been discussed
with the Directorate of Intelligence. Comments or
queries are invited and may be directed to the
author James ⬛⬛⬛⬛ Analytic Group, National
Intelligence Council, on ⬛⬛⬛⬛⬛⬛⬛
⬛⬛⬛⬛⬛⬛

Top Secret
NIC M 83-10006
⬛⬛⬛⬛
April 1983

Preface

This paper presents the preliminary findings of an examination of all known reports of civil unrest in the USSR from 1970 through 1982. Some of the findings may challenge our image of the Soviet Union as an effectively repressed society. Thus, the larger significance of civil unrest in the USSR requires additional systematic and ongoing study by the Intelligence Community. This paper focuses primarily on defining and measuring civil unrest rather than attempting to assess its full implications. (U)

Civil unrest as defined in this paper does not, for the most part, involve the activities of dissident Soviet intellectuals whose efforts have been widely reported in the world's press. Rather, it refers to a broad range of actions by individuals belonging to a much wider mass of the Soviet public, who are either protesting specific policies of various levels of the Soviet government that affect them personally or who participate in spontaneous disorders even though they know that such action is strictly forbidden. We categorize and define these protest actions as follows:

- *Strike.* A collective action by workers at a jobsite to curtail economic production in support of specific objectives requiring redress by management to resolve.

- *Demonstration.* An activity of persons publicly assembled, or otherwise publicly identified, to protest a government policy or to advance a cause not supported by the government.

- *Riot.* A protest action that results in a temporary breakdown of public order involving property damage or injuries or that requires the mobilization of armed force to restore order.

- *Political Violence.* Acts of or attempts at violence in which political motives are readily apparent or can easily be inferred, including assassination of political leaders or state officials, self-immolation, and sabotage of state functions. (U)

Approximately 280 reported incidents from 1970 to the present are the data on which this analysis is based. These incidents do not necessarily indicate the existence of great subterranean political dissension or represent any acute threat to the regime. For Western democracies, some 280 events spanning more than a decade would represent nothing significant. Throughout Soviet history, however, public political activity, such as

iii

Top Secret

[p ii blank]

protests and demonstrations, has been considered illegal and politically impermissible. Under Andropov, no less than his predecessors, *any* public protester takes a significant risk, no matter how peaceful the act, and at the very least must expect harsh treatment by the militia, including immediate arrest or forceable dispersal. Repeat offenders and strike leaders can expect a combination of KGB harassment, loss of pay or jobs, longer prison terms, forced labor, or confinement in mental institutions. The fact that civil unrest nonetheless occurs in the face of these constraints indicates the existence of a problem of some consequence for the USSR's leaders; at a minimum, Soviet elites are indeed more concerned now about the potential effects of popular discontent than they have been for the past 25 years or so.

Because these incidents represent a political problem for Soviet authorities, virtually no information about them is available from public Soviet sources. We are aware that reporting validity—knowing that an event actually happened as the report states—is a nagging problem in research of this type.[1] Most of the reports for this study have come from a variety of HUMINT sources: diplomatic reporting, travelers, emigres, defectors, and sensitive human sources.

Few of the incidents in this study can be considered "proven conclusively" in the sense that they have been reported by multiple, independent sources. We have used only those reports that appear to be credible, however, and we believe that the data base as a whole is reasonably sound.

Finally, the data base represents a thorough but undoubtedly incomplete compilation of incidents of civil unrest. In back-searching available reports for the period 1970-80, some have surely been missed. For 1981 and 1982 the compilation of available reports is probably more complete, but it is very likely that a larger proportion of incidents for these past two years is not yet covered in available reporting. This gap results necessarily from the time lag that occurs between actual events and subsequent reports that identify them. Nevertheless, if allowances are made for the uncertainties of reporting, the data base compiled for this study should provide a good approximation of the extent and nature of civil unrest in the Soviet Union since 1970.

In sum, care should be taken neither to overestimate the significance and potential of this study's data nor to assume that the cited examples have negligible political importance to the Soviet regime.

[1] For a more detailed discussion of data validity and related methodological issues, see the appendix.

Dimensions of Civil Unrest
in the Soviet Union

Key Judgments

*Information available
as of 25 March 1983
was used in this Memorandum.*

Civil unrest in the Soviet Union takes many forms. Since 1970 intelligence
sources report over 280 cases of industrial strikes and work stoppages,
public demonstrations, and occasional violence, including sabotage, rioting,
and even political assassination attempts. Virtually none of these incidents
has been reported in the Soviet media, and only a few in the Western press.
If there is error in the estimated total number of these incidents, it is
almost certainly on the low side because of underreporting.[1]

Such unrest is geographically widespread. Reported incidents have occurred in close to 100 Soviet cities (or oblasts) and in almost every republic
during the past decade—from the Baltics to Siberia, Central Asia to the
Arctic; in large cities, small towns, and rural areas. Apparently no place is
immune: disturbances have occurred in huge factories and small plants,
coal mines and food stores, and at government buildings and Communist
Party headquarters.

A wide cross section of the Soviet populace, including industrial workers,
coal miners, bus drivers, and construction crews, has been involved in civil
unrest. In several instances, white collar workers, union leaders, families,
and Party members also have been involved.

Much civil unrest is economically based. In particular, food shortages and
dissatisfaction with the quality of life in the USSR account for more
incidents of unrest than any other factor. Because consumer frustrations
are rooted in the budgetary priorities of the regime and the inherent
sluggishness of the Soviet economy and bureaucracy, they are not likely to
subside in the near term.

The combination of economic grievances with ethnic nationalism in the
non-Russian republics (especially in the Baltic states) accounts for most of
the incidents of civil unrest observed since 1970 and for most of the
apparent increase in unrest during the past four years.

---

[1] These data and the problem of underreporting have been discussed with CIA's Methodolo-
gy Center, Analytic Support Group, whose view, based on an appropriate statistical model
for this kind of problem, is that the actual number of incidents of unrest for the period is at
least double the reported 280 cases (see text and appendix for elaboration).

v

Top Secret

ORCON

In general, the regime has been careful to discriminate between strike actions and other forms of unrest, particularly if the issue is food shortages Limited information suggests that striking workers are more likely to win concessions than demonstrators; the latter are much more likely to be arrested or dispersed.

Even though political violence in the USSR is neither widespread nor organized, scattered reports since the late 1970s of sabotage, arson, and political assassination attempts suggest a depth of commitment in some antisystem individuals that has not been evident in earlier years. More than most kinds of civil unrest, political violence shatters tranquility and introduces a note of unpredictability in challenges to the public order.

The regime is known to be concerned about the disruptive potential of civil unrest. Crash efforts to buy off striking workers with food supplies instead of outright repression, the scale of the food program itself, and various expressions of concern by midlevel and higher political elites as seen in HUMINT source reporting point to an apparent sensitivity that anything resembling a Polish-type Solidarity movement must not be permitted to develop.

The scope and character of popular grievances that are suggested in recent civil unrest probably present a greater long-range challenge to the regime than the narrower intellectual dissident movement. These incidents of civil unrest imply a popular willingness to hold the regime more accountable for perceived shortcomings. Moreover, the spontaneity inherent in much of the unrest examined here may complicate the maintenance of public order. Further, a policy response primarily based on repression may be more likely to cause additional popular alienation than to reduce it. Such an outcome would undermine current Soviet efforts to increase substantially labor productivity, one of the government's most important economic priorities. For the Soviets, this may be a vicious circle of greater potential domestic significance for the 1980s than the regime has had to cope with anytime in the past three decades.

**Director of
Central
Intelligence**

25X1

Possible Soviet Responses to the US Strategic Defense Initiative

Interagency Intelligence Assessment

MEMORANDUM FOR: DCI 2 7 JUN 1984

As you prepare for your NSPG on Tuesday, I thought you might find this of use for the weekend.

Date   22 June 84

FORM 101 USE PREVIOUS
5-75   EDITIONS

25X1

Secret

NIC M 83-10017
12 September 1983

Copy 459

25X1

PREFACE

On 23 March 1983, President Reagan called for a comprehensive and intensive effort to define a long-term research and development program to begin to achieve the ultimate goal of eliminating the threat posed by strategic nuclear missiles.

Though the media have given considerable attention to the issue and have focused attention on exotic space-based beam weapons—the so-called Star Wars systems—the President did not specifically mention any weapon concepts or basing:

— Ballistic missile defense systems could be on air, ground, and submarine platforms as well as on satellites; high-energy lasers, particle beams, or microwave systems could become elements of a national ballistic missile defense (BMD) system along with improved conventional-technology systems.

It appears likely that any strategic defense scheme will involve some combination of systems in a layered defense. A space-based directed energy weapon may be used to destroy enemy ballistic missiles in their boost phase; ground-based or space-based lasers or conventional weapons may be used to destroy buses and reentry vehicles in midcourse; ground-based beam weapons, missile interceptors, and other weapons may be used to provide terminal defense.

In attempting to neutralize the development and deployment of a ballistic missile defense by the United States, the Soviets will be able to select from a range of technical, diplomatic, military, political propaganda, and clandestine measures. Since this range is broad, and since the time scale (20 to 30 years) of the proposed US BMD effort extends well beyond anyone's ability to make accurate forecasts, we can claim no precision in evaluating the Soviets' course of action. We have instead focused on general principles and constraints in the areas of politics, military doctrine, and Soviet research and development practices that will influence their response to a US BMD system. Subsequently, we identified a variety of military and technological options the Soviets could make at various times in the future. No attempt has been made to perform evaluations as to the relative advantages of one kind of system or device over another.

Note: This paper was prepared under the auspices of the National Intelligence Officer for Strategic Programs. It was submitted in support of [   ] an interagency report in response to the President's strategic defense initiative [   ] This paper was coordinated at the working level by the Central Intelligence Agency and the Defense Intelligence Agency.

25X1
25X1

SECRET

25X1

SUMMARY

In the near term, we expect the Soviets to rely principally on a concerted political and diplomatic effort first to force the United States to drop its ballistic missile defense (BMD) plans or, failing that, to negotiate them away. There are also certain limited military steps the Soviets could take initially for the purpose of improving their bargaining position and for preparing them for initial US deployment should it occur.

Over the long term, if the United States goes ahead with plans to develop and deploy its defensive system the Soviets will have a different set of problems. Assuming they know the likely structure and capabilities of US defensive forces, they will look for effective technical countermeasures.

It appears that there will be a large variety of possible measures the Soviets can choose from to preserve the viability of their ballistic missile forces. Intercontinental ballistic missiles (ICBMs) and submarine-launched ballistic missiles (SLBMs) can be upgraded with new boosters, decoys, penetration aids, and multiple warheads. The signatures of these systems can be reduced and new launch techniques and basing schemes can be devised which make them less vulnerable to US missile warning and defensive weapon systems. These systems can also be hardened or modified to reduce their vulnerability to directed energy weapons.

The Soviets can employ other offensive systems, particularly manned bombers and long-range cruise missiles with improved penetration aids and stealth technologies, to assume a greater burden of the strategic offensive strike role and to exploit the weaknesses in US air defense capabilities.

The Soviets can continue development and deployment of their own ballistic missile defense systems. The Moscow antiballistic missile system can be expanded and improved, and a more widespread system deployed, with additional launchers, improved missile detection and tracking capabilities, and more capable interceptors. The Soviets can expand their ongoing efforts on directed energy weapons, weapons which also provide antisatellite capabilities which could be used against some space-based elements of a US BMD system. In most of the directed energy weapons technologies, the Soviets are now on a par with, or lead, the United States. They are likely to pursue these efforts

25X1

regardless of whether the United States sustains its strategic defense initiative.

We believe it is highly unlikely that the Soviets will undertake a "crash" program in reaction to US BMD developments, but rather will seek to counter them by steadily paced efforts over the decades the United States will need to develop and deploy its overall defense. They will look for solutions that are least disruptive to their way of doing business and involve the least possible change to their planned programs. The Soviets are not likely to embrace a fundamental shift in the strategic environment entailing reliance on strategic defenses by both sides.

The Soviets could choose to allocate the necessary R&D resources and could obtain some flexibility for new types of deployment by adjusting other programs. They are likely to encounter technical and manufacturing problems in developing and deploying more advanced systems. If they attempted to deploy new advanced systems not presently planned, while continuing their overall planned force modernization, significant additional levels of spending would be required.[1] This would place substantial additional pressures on the Soviet economy and confront the leadership with difficult policy choices.

If, through some set of circumstances, the Soviets were faced with actual or impending deployment of a US system and had no effective military counter to it, we think there are various possibilities for Soviet actions, ranging from major arms control concessions, to threats of military action in other areas, to threatened attacks on space-based components of a US system, to sabotage against US facilities. In some extreme scenarios, the Soviets could carry out a massive attack against the US defensive system, although we think that to be highly unlikely, given the near certainty of thereby initiating general war with the United States.

---

[1] The Soviets have extensive efforts in the advanced technology area applicable to strategic defense, but we do not know to what extent these are planned for deployment.

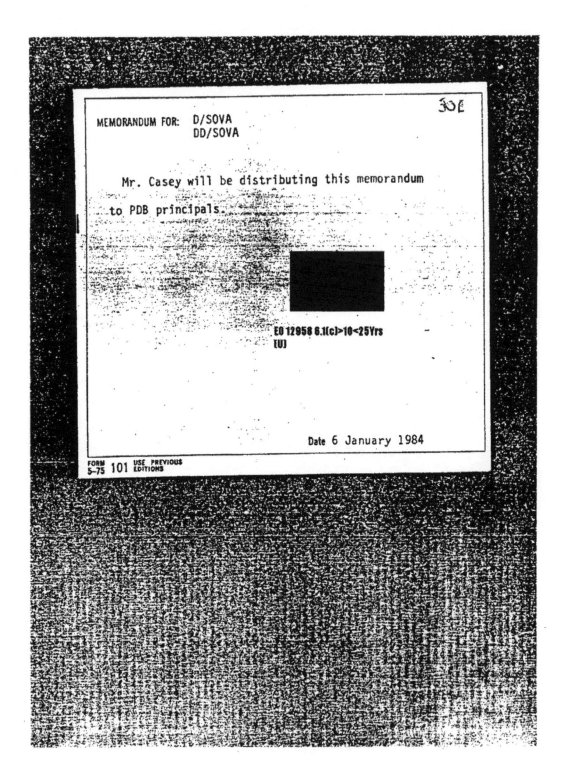

MEMORANDUM FOR: D/SOVA
DD/SOVA

Mr. Casey will be distributing this memorandum
to PDB principals.

EO 12958 6.1(c)>10<25Yrs
[U]

Date 6 January 1984

FORM
5-75 101 USE PREVIOUS
EDITIONS

5

SECRET

Central Intelligence Agency

Washington D.C. 20505

DIRECTORATE OF INTELLIGENCE

30 December 1983

Soviet Thinking on the Possibility

of Armed Confrontation with the United States

→ *Jack Matlock*
This is almost
congruent to
my analysis,
What do
you think?

Bud

1-10-84

Summary

Contrary to the impression conveyed by Soviet propaganda, Moscow does not appear to anticipate a near-term military confrontation with the United States. With the major exception of the Middle East, there appears to be no region in which the Soviets are now apprehensive that action in support of clients could lead to Soviet-American armed collision. By playing up the "war danger," Moscow hopes to encourage resistance to INF deployment in Western Europe, deepen cleavages within the Atlantic alliance, and increase public pressure in the United States for a more conciliatory posture toward the USSR. ▪

Soviet policymakers, however, almost certainly are very concerned that trends they foresee in long-term US military programs could in time erode the USSR's military gains of the past fifteen years, heighten US political leverage, and perhaps increase the chances of confrontation. ▪

This memorandum was prepared by ▮▮▮▮▮▮▮▮
▮▮▮▮▮▮ Office of Soviet Analysis.

WARNING NOTICE --
Intelligence Sources or
Methods Involved

CL BY ▮▮▮▮
DECL OADR
DERIVED FROM FOR 9-82

SECRET

NOFORN NOCONTRACT UNINTEL ORCON

~~SECRET~~

The Director of Central Intelligence

Washington, D.C. 20505

Executive Registry
85- 2565

27 June 1985

Dear Mr. President,

You may find this good airplane reading.

It is a good picture of Gorbachev's style, objectives and operating methods as shown in the first 100 days of his leadership.

You will sympathize with his targetting the massive bureaucratic apparatus,

Respectfully yours,

William J. Casey

The President
The White House
Washington, D. C. 20500

ALL WITH ATTACHMENT

Orig - The President
1 - DCI
1 - DDCI
1 - DDI
1 - D/SOVA
1 - ER File

Approved for Release by CIA
Date Jan 2011

~~SECRET~~

SECRET

Central Intelligence Agency

(b) (1) (b) (3)

Washington, D.C. 20505

DIRECTORATE OF INTELLIGENCE

JUNE 1985

Gorbachev, the New Broom

Summary

Gorbachev has demonstrated in his first 100 days that he is the most aggressive and activist Soviet leader since Khrushchev. He is willing to take controversial and even unpopular decisions-- like the antialcohol campaign--and to break with recent precedent by criticizing the actions of his colleagues on the Politburo.

He has thrown down the gauntlet on issues as controversial as the allocation of investment, broadgauged management reform, and purging the system of incompetent and corrupt officials. The very insistence of his rhetoric allows little room for compromise or retreat.

Gorbachev is gambling that an attack on corruption and inefficiency, not radical reform, will turn the domestic situation around. While a risky course, his prospects for success should not be underestimated. Although his approach is controversial, his near term prospects look good. Unlike his immediate predecessors, he has already managed to firm up his base of support in the Politburo and Secretariat. He can also count on some support from middle level officials of the bureaucracy who were frustrated by the stagnation of the Brezhnev era. The public as well has responded favorably to his style, judging by initial reaction

This paper was prepared by [   ] of the Office of Soviet Analysis. Comments and questions may be directed to the Chief, [   ]

SECRET

APPROVED FOR
RELEASE DATE:
18-Nov-2008

Intelligence

Gorbachev's Economic Agenda: Promises, Potentials, and Pitfalls

An Intelligence Assessment

Gorbachev's Economic Agenda: Promises, Potentials, and Pitfalls

Key Judgments

Information available as of 6 September 1985 was used in this report.

Since coming to power, Mikhail Gorbachev has set in motion the most aggressive economic agenda since the Khrushchev era. The key elements are:

- A reallocation of investment resources aimed at accelerating S&T and modernizing the country's stock of plant and equipment.
- A revitalization of management and planning to rid the Soviet bureaucracy of incompetence and petty tutelage and put more operational control of enterprises in the hands of managers on the scene.
- A renewal of Andropov's anticorruption and discipline campaigns, coupled with a new temperance campaign, to increase and perhaps improve worker effort.

All of Gorbachev's initiatives are aimed at raising productivity and efficiency throughout the economy by matching more and better equipment with a motivated work force and an enlightened managerial cadre. He has put his finger on the very tasks that the economy has never done well and has become progressively less able to do as it has grown in size and complexity.

Although Soviet economic performance has improved in recent years from the low levels of 1979-82, Gorbachev still faces an economy that cannot simultaneously maintain rapid growth in defense spending, satisfy demand for greater quantity and variety of consumer goods and services, invest the amounts required for economic modernization and expansion, and continue to support client-state economies. Gorbachev, in our view, has a clear understanding of these limitations; he is obviously extremely impatient that they be addressed now.

Soviet officialdom probably was caught offguard by Gorbachev's sweeping condemnation of past economic policies, particularly considering the recent economic rebound, and was surprised that he apparently was ready to take action so early in his tenure. Despite the urgency of his rhetoric, he seems aware that implementing his programs too rapidly carries substantial economic and political risks:

- He has prepared the party and bureaucracy for substantial change by bluntly laying out the need for management reorganization and renewal, but has yet to provide specific details on controversial issues that would provide a basis for organized resistance.
- He has moved aggressively to replace old-line economic managers but has yet to replace Council of Ministers Chairman Tikhonov, regarded by most Soviets as a major political obstacle to economic change.

iii

September 1985

- He has talked about the potential need for "profound" changes in the area of economic reform, while strongly supporting the need to maintain central control. ▮

Program specifics will be announced by next February along, we judge, with Tikhonov's replacement. It is unlikely that they will contain any radical departures from what Gorbachev has already announced. At present his game plan seems to be a realistic assessment of what can be done in the short run while planning and developing a consensus for more radical change over the long haul if.he deems that it is needed ▮

Success with the initial stages of Gorbachev's program could provide a relatively immediate growth dividend that could be used to bolster worker morale and underwrite future growth. How much economic improvement will occur and how long it can be sustained, however, is very much an open question. Modernization is slow by nature in any economic system and in the Soviet case will run into the perennial conflict between meeting output goals and reequipping enterprises with new equipment and technology. Streamlining the bureaucracy will be resisted by countless officials whose jobs and perquisites are threatened, and a new set of incentives must be instituted to motivate a new type of Soviet manager. Discipline campaigns can go only so far in energizing a cynical work force. ▮

Gorbachev will be hard pressed to find the resources necessary to underwrite his modernization goals. The economic dividend from management reforms and the discipline campaign will not substantially relieve the basic scarcity of resources nor obviate the need for fundamental systemic change:

- Improving worker morale and management effectiveness will require an effective incentive system and a greater availability of high-quality consumer goods at a time when the investment sector will be oriented toward producer goods and new defense programs will be coming on line. In fact, Gorbachev's investment program implies a potential decline of some 60 percent in the investment increment going to consumer-oriented sectors.

- The regime's plan to hold energy's share of investment constant comes at a time when demand for energy will grow and the cost of offsetting declining oil production will be rapidly rising. If the requisite investment is not forthcoming, the current decline in oil production could become precipitous.

iv

- The increased managerial independence necessary to spur effective
  technological development and utilization is inconsistent with a centrally
  planned pricing and allocation system, leading to the likelihood of
  management disillusionment and subsequent reversion to the very
  methods that have led to waste, fraud, and mismanagement for years.

Gorbachev could employ various options to address these issues, but all
contain serious pitfalls. East European countries could be ordered to
shoulder a larger part of the economic burden, including increased exports
of equipment to the USSR, but their own deep economic problems increase
the likelihood of confrontation between Moscow and its allies. A drive to
increase imports of Western technology would come at a time when the
prospects for expanding hard currency exports, particularly oil, look dim. A
shift of resources from defense to civilian uses could have considerable
positive impact over the long run, but even the suggestion of such a shift
might damage Gorbachev's relations with the military and risk deep
divisions within the Politburo. Finally, major economic reforms to promote
managerial effectiveness would encounter strong resistance on political and
ideological grounds, particularly since they threaten the institutional
prerogatives and thus the privileged position of the Soviet elite.

Indications that Gorbachev has decided on and gained consensus for more
radical changes could include:

- New, dramatic initiatives to reach an accord at Geneva and concrete
  proposals for reduced tensions at the November meeting between the US
  President and the General Secretary, which might signal a willingness
  and desire to reduce the Soviet resource commitment to defense and
  create an atmosphere for expanded commerce with the West.

- Select legalization of private-sector activity, particularly in regard to
  consumer services, which would indicate a willingness to confront past
  economic orthodoxy in order to improve consumer welfare and thereby
  economic performance.

- Breaking the monopoly of the foreign trade apparatus, which would
  signal an increased reliance on managerial independence at some cost to
  centralized control.

v

Continued reliance on marginal tinkering despite clear indications that the plan for economic revitalization is faltering would indicate that Gorbachev, like Brezhnev before him, has succumbed to a politically expedient but economically ineffective approach. ▮

vi

21942   **2 7 SEP 1988**

MEMORANDUM FOR: Richard Kerr
                  Deputy Director for Intelligence

FROM: Douglas J. MacEachin
                  Director of Soviet Analysis

SUBJECT: Leadership Situation in the USSR

1. The increasingly volatile situation in the USSR makes an already difficult analytical problem even more uncertain. On the one hand, forecasts of impending political crisis for Gorbachev—particularly given the great political skills he has demonstrated to date—run the risk of being perceived as alarmist. Yet his radical program is placing such enormous stress on the Soviet system, damaging the vested interests of so many powerful institutional elites, and creating such a high degree of tension in society as a whole that failure to call attention to the potential for leadership conflict to come to a head would reflect a gravely unjustified complacence.

2. This memorandum lays out the factors that account for our unease about our ability to forecast developments in the Soviet leadership. It was drafted by   , Chief   Division, but it reflects the views of our cadre of senior Kremlin watchers as a whole. We are loath to assign probabilities to various scenarios, and our analysts do not agree among themselves about whether a showdown will take place, much less about who will triumph if it does. Academic Sovietologists are equally uncertain about these questions.

3. Given the importance that a leadership upheaval could have for US national interests, if you agree with this assessment you may want to forward the memo to the DCI with a recommendation that he consider passing it on to key policymakers.

                                   Douglas J. MacEachin

Attachment:

Prospects for a Leadership Crisis

The renewal of large-scale unrest in the Caucasus comes at a time when Gorbachev is beleaguered with mounting economic problems and growing political opposition to his policies. He has had some recent successes in moving his reform agenda forward, but his very successes are alienating many elites at all levels of the system. There is a good chance that Gorbachev will accomodate his Politburo critics by backing off from some of his radical proposals for change. Given the depth of divisions in the Politburo, however, there are increasing prospects that conflict will come to a head. Neither the timing nor the outcome of such a confrontation are possible to predict with any precision. The leadership appears to be pulling together to bring the current crisis situation in the Caucasus under control, but the conflagration there could lead to further polarization within the leadership that will later result in a denouement.

A sizeable portion of the Soviet Politburo--including Ligachev, Chebrikov, Solomentsev, Gromyko, and Shcherbitskiy--have good reason for wanting to be rid of Gorbachev. There appear to be differences among these leaders on some policy issues and they do not necessarily constitute a cohesive coalition at present. But all of them must feel personally threatened by Gorbachev's plans and they now seem to share a belief that the Gorbachev "cure" for the USSR is worse than the "disease;" they fear his program will erode the old foundations of party rule before solid new foundations are built.

The burgeoning of nationality unrest has been a key factor leading some of Gorbachev's Politburo peers to conclude that his overall strategy in domestic policy is fundamentally flawed. In addition to the breakdown of order in Armenia and Azerbaijan and an acute situation in the Baltic, demonstrations took place last week in Georgia and last month in the Ukraine--the largest and most important non-Russian republic.

, it is abundantly clear to nationality greivances. Ideologically orthodox leaders are undoubtedly repelled by a policy toward the Baltic republics that smacks of appeasement, however hard Gorbahcev may attempt to portray concessions to national interests there as necessary to coopt moderates and head off a lurch toward separatism. Strong backlash sentiment is growing among conservative Russian nationalists, and Ligachev is acting as their champion.

Elsewhere in the Bloc, conservative leaders are concerned that Gorbachev's policies will complicate political control problems. In particular, the public pressure that the Soviet regime recently exerted on the Poles to take a softer line in dealing with Solidarity makes Gorbachev open to accusations of adopting a capitulatory stance that will encourage opposition activity. One

1

item in the bill of indictment against Khrushchev was that his policies were antagonizing conservative East European regimes. If the situation in Poland should continue to degenerate--or if the situation should get out of control of the authorities in any of the East European countries--it would now be a powerful weapon in the hand of Gorbachev's opponents.

Much of the Soviet party bureaucracy is up in arms over Gorbachev's attack on their privileges, his drive to cut back the size of the apparatus, and his effort to infuse the elite with new blood by opening up the election process somewhat. Some special stores for the elite were closed in early September. If the procedures used in recently concluded elections at the lowest rung of the party are followed in the upcoming regional elections, officials at that level face the prospect of losing their sinecures to secret ballots and competition from rival candidates in many cases. Moreover, a party spokesman said recently that the number of officials working in the CPSU Central Committee apparatus would be slashed by half, and similar reductions are planned for the republics. In this environment, many party officials look to Ligachev as their protector.

The trial of Brezhnev's son-in-law Churbanov, and the accompanying escalation of media condemnation of the Brezhnev leadership, is a major source of disquietude for members of the Brezhnev Old Guard still on the Politburo. Reformers at the June Party Conference attacked Gromyko and Solomentsev by name and a liberal Soviet journalist recently criticized Shcherbitskiy in an interview with a European newsman. A scathing critique of Brezhnev published in September in Literary Gazette openly acknowledged that Brezhnev was in effect a surrogate for leaders who are still in office.

A media campaign directed against excessive secrecy on the part of the KGB has undoubtedly brought home to Chebrikov that he is on Gorbachev's hit list as well. Since his Dzerzhinskiy Day speech a year ago made clear that Chebrikov had thrown in his lot with Ligachev, Chebrikov has looked for opportunities to cast aspersions on Gorbachev's policies. Most recently, in an August interview, he challenged the ideological underpinnings of Gorbachev's foreign policy and let it be known that the glasnost he favors takes the form of publicizing information about subversive activities of Western intelligence services inside the USSR. We believe that Chebrikov would almost certainly participate in any leadership coup against Gorbachev that he thought had a reasonably good chance of succeeding.

Gorbachev appears to have reached something of a modus vivendi with the military, and media pillorying of the military has virtually stopped. Both General Staff Chief Akhromeyev and Defense Minister Yazov have actively supported his arms control strategy so far.

2

DECLASSIFIED INTELLIGENCE DOCUMENTS | 57

Gorbachev has also provided ammunition to opponents eager to portray him as a leader with an inflated ego, excessive personal ambition, a tendency to make highhanded decisions, and a penchant for demagogic behavior. Some Soviet officials view his walkabouts as unseemly efforts to imitate the self-promotion techniques of Western politicians. Eyebrows have been raised by the limelight accorded Raisa as the Soviet "First Lady." Gorbachev's efforts to please the crowd by bashing the bureaucracy do not endear him to the nomenklatura. Many Soviets regard Gorbachev's proposal to combine the top state and party jobs as a blatant power grab; even Gorbachev admirers such as Roy Medvedev were reminded of Khrushchev's "harebrained schemes."

On the economic reform front, Gorbachev has scored some recent victories in terms of preparing the way for getting approval of desired legislation--for example, reduce state orders for enterprises and to reject high tax rates for cooperatives. He has made major new proposals for agricultural reform--especially the use of long-term leasing arrangements to expand the scope of private initiative in farming. Yet implementation of reforms already adopted proceeds slowly, and major economic actors feel threatened by them. Most factory managers fear they will sink if forced to sink or swim. Most of the powerful ministerial bureaucracy resents being left with considerable responsibility but reduced authority. Most of the industrial working class fears the loss of guaranteed job benefits and security.

Gorbachev so far has not achieved any significant improvement in the overall economic situation, and there is a widespread perception that living conditions are deteriorating. The General Secretary is trying to reach out to new constituencies to counter elite resistance to his program, and there is no question that he has caught the imagination of many patriotic, enterprising citizens at all levels of the society--people who believe they and the country will benefit from a more competitive economic environment and a less repressive political system. But growing distress over the standard of living is reducing the attractiveness of perestroyka even for this "strong" minority of the population. Gorbachev has evidently succeeded in winning approval for a diversion of resources to the consumer sector in the annual plan. At this point, however, the only major element of the population enthusiastically behind his reform program is the intelligentsia. Even if he is able to build a broader popular base of support, his ability to mobilize this diffuse support very effectively will be limited until reforms that expand participation in the political process are implemented.

On the plus side, Gorbachev continues to enjoy major political advantages. As General Secretary, he has been able to dominate the policy agenda and pack the Secretariat with supporters. Although he has had more difficulty making changes in the Politburo, he does have powerful allies in that body--including Yakovlev and Shevardnadze--as well as less reliable backing from a number of members who have found it politically expedient so far to follow his lead.

3

The most important source of his strength has been a leadership consensus that a new course for the country is necessary to avoid economic stagnation, the decline of the USSR as a global power, and a growth in societal alienation that could produce political instability down the road. Gorbachev has succeeded in preventing any other member of the political leadership from fully articulating a program that could serve as a viable alternative to his course, and by now the old Brezhnev order has been so thoroughly discredited that turning back the clock very far would be extremely difficult. Moreover, considering how much turmoil exists in the country today and how much the public's respect for the regime's will and ability to use coercion has diminished, many leaders may fear that attempting to remove Gorbachev could touch off widespread unrest. Finally, even his opponents realize that Gorbachev has had enormous success in foreign policy, managing to blur if not to obliterate the USSR's "enemy image" in the West, and that removing him could undo much of what has been achieved internationally. Nevertheless, these strengths do not guarantee the success of his policies or his ability to retain his office if the perception of serious disorder and misbegotten policies continues.

The problems facing Gorbachev are so serious that he may well take the course of political accomodation. He cannot compromise too far on fundamental parts of his program without causing an overall loss of momentum and the beginning of a process of piecemeal political defeat. But he is not a Yeltsin; he has shown a capacity for tactical retreat in the face of strong resistance, and a preference at times for political manuever over direct confrontation.

On balance, however, we believe there is a greater chance that events will move toward a dramatic resolution. Politburo members appear to have closed ranks in dealing with the situation in the Caucasus, which poses an unprecedented challenge for the leadership as a whole. But over the next year, given the key positions held by some of the leaders opposing Gorbachev, the fact that a large portion of the Central Commmittee shares their fears and concerns, and the existence of reservations about Gorbachev within the KGB and military establishment, there is a good chance that they will move against Gorbachev or that Gorbachev himself will risk a preemptive move to consolidate his power. Any showdown at this level, in the midst of such a volatile political situation, would carry grave risks for all involved. It could involve Gorbachev's removal from his position but it could also result in his resounding success--similar to Khrushchev's expulsion of the "anti-party group" in 1957.

Directorate of
Intelligence

Rising Political Instability
Under Gorbachev:
Understanding the Problem and
Prospects for Resolution

An Intelligence Assessment

Reverse Blank

April 1989

Rising Political Instability Under Gorbachev: Understanding the Problem and Prospects for Resolution

Key Judgments

Information available as of 31 March 1989 was used in this report.

The Soviet Union is less stable today than at any time since Stalin's great purges in the 1930s. General Secretary Gorbachev clearly hopes that, by shaking up the Soviet system, he can rouse the population out of its lethargy and channel the forces he is releasing in a constructive direction. Even Gorbachev realizes, however, that it is far from certain that he will be able to control the process he has set in motion. That process could create so much turmoil and unrest that it will be very difficult for him to achieve his goals. In the extreme, his policies and political power could be undermined, and the political stability of the Soviet system could be fundamentally threatened.

Gorbachev's reforms—while yet to remedy existing problems—have caused new challenges to surface. Having seen their quality of life stagnate under Gorbachev, Soviet citizens are becoming increasingly skeptical of reform, seeing it more and more as a threat to the secure existence they recall they enjoyed under Brezhnev. Moreover, the aspects of reform that are potentially most destabilizing are only in their early stages. The political reforms being introduced could further erode central authority and could give disaffected groups new platforms to challenge the regime. Radical economic reform appears further away because the kinds of market-oriented measures required to meet economic objectives would heighten social tensions by raising prices, creating unemployment, and increasing economic inequality. Moreover, such a transition could create a period of economic chaos and a sharp drop in production before the reforms began to yield positive results.

Over the past two years, incidents of political unrest in the USSR, ranging from benign small gatherings to major acts of political violence, have sharply escalated. Under the banner of *glasnost*, Soviet citizens are organizing groups that could form the basis of a political opposition and are advancing a wide range of demands that challenge central authority. The most dangerous of these are the nationalist movements that have blossomed in many republics, unleashing centrifugal forces that, if unchecked, could threaten to tear the system apart. This increasing assertiveness by national minorities is provoking a backlash among the Russians, emboldening Russian nationalist groups and setting the stage for violent clashes in the republics where the Russians are in danger of becoming second-rate citizens.

April 1989

The comprehensive nature of Gorbachev's reforms has polarized the Soviet elite, alienating many party members who stand to lose privileges and social stature and increasing the potential for a debilitating split in the leadership. Party conservatives fear that the cure being offered by Gorbachev is worse than the disease, arguing that the reforms may undermine party rule and produce a crisis of their own. Although the influence of Gorbachev's opponents on the Politburo has been weakened, they have a strong base of support among members of the elite who feel threatened by his reforms, including sizable elements in the Central Committee, the party and state apparatus, the military, and the KGB. ■■■■

There have also been growing signs of frustration among Soviet citizens. Reforms are fueling expectations for improvements in the quality of life, but, from the standpoint of the Soviet workers, Gorbachev's economic program has been a near disaster, and there is a widespread popular perception that conditions have deteriorated. Moreover, the secure existence they came to take for granted under Brezhnev is being threatened by pressures to work harder and a fear that only the most productive workers will be rewarded. *Glasnost* and political liberalization have enhanced regime legitimacy among some elements of the population, especially the intelligentsia, by giving them hope that things can be improved by working through the system. At the same time, as the 26 March election demonstrated, such reforms have released pressures for further changes that could undermine the party's monopoly on political power. ■■■

Nevertheless, the Soviet leadership has undertaken the hazardous path of radical reform because it believes that the old system was failing and that, in the long run, it would have been more dangerous to do nothing. Particularly while Gorbachev remains at the helm, the leadership will not be easily swayed from this path. It specifically recognizes that the highly centralized Stalinist economic model was increasingly ill suited to reversing the economic slide that began under Brezhnev and narrowing the technological gap with the West. At the same time, Soviet political institutions were failing to provide social liberties and legitimate channels for airing concerns to a population that is increasingly well educated and informed. Corruption, abuses of privilege, and unfulfilled promises under Brezhnev compounded these problems by increasing popular cynicism and alienation and helping to erode the legitimacy of the regime. ■■■

iv

The Soviet leadership possesses tremendous capabilities for controlling unrest and preventing opposition from threatening the regime. Gorbachev himself is a major asset, demonstrating masterful political skills in building support for his radical agenda, keeping the opposition off balance, and maintaining cohesion in the leadership. He is also a risk taker, however, increasing the possibility he could miscalculate in a critical situation. Should political skill alone not be sufficient to control opposition, the regime still possesses the powerful coercive forces of the KGB, military, and militia. While it has already used these to deal with particular outbreaks of unrest, any broad-scale reliance on coercion to maintain stability would seriously undermine the reform process. Short of resorting to force, the considerable degree of centralized control the Soviet state exerts over key aspects of society—jobs, prices, wages, housing, transportation, media, and imports—gives it other important levers it can use to help maintain stability. ■

The next several years promise to be some of the most turbulent in Soviet history. Indeed, while the kind of turmoil now being created in the USSR has been effectively managed in many countries, in other countries it has contributed to the destabilization of the political system. There are too many unknowns to determine whether Gorbachev will be able to control the process he has started, or if it will increasingly come to control him, making a wide range of outcomes possible over the next five years:

• If Gorbachev's reforms begin to produce tangible results and if he is lucky, he should remain in power and prevent any of the potential problems he faces from getting out of control, while continuing to move his reforms ahead.

• A growing perception within the leadership that reforms are threatening the stability of the regime could lead to a conservative reaction. This would probably, but not necessarily, involve a transfer of power—with a majority of the Politburo voting Gorbachev out, as happened with Khrushchev in 1964—and a repudiation of many aspects of reform.

• Those pressing for a maximalist agenda could gain control of the political system as a result of democratization and *glasnost*—as happened in Czechoslovakia in 1968—and force Gorbachev out.

- Should a sharp polarization of the leadership prevent it from acting resolutely to deal with a growing crisis, the prospects would increase for a conservative coup involving a minority of Politburo members supported by elements of the military and KGB. The prospects of a unilateral military coup are much more remote.

- If ethnic problems mount, consumer and worker discontent grow, and divisions in the leadership prevent it from acting decisively, organized political opposition could threaten the regime. Under these conditions, opposition groups could come to share power, as Solidarity did in Poland in the early 1980s, or individual republics might win de facto independence. ▮▮▮

To get through this difficult period, the Soviet leadership can be expected to continue to place a high premium on creating a stable and predictable environment—minimizing the possibility of threats to Soviet interests from abroad. East-West relations, especially with the United States, will be particularly important. To help ease the strain on the economy and improve the prospects for delivering on promises to the consumer, the Soviet leadership will continue to vigorously pursue arms control and seek ways to reduce military spending. ▮▮▮

Gorbachev can be expected to seek more foreign policy successes to enhance his legitimacy, build his personal prestige, and distract attention from domestic problems. For this and other reasons, he can therefore be expected to maintain a very high profile in the international arena, continuing to advance major foreign policy initiatives. At times, however, domestic crises—some of which may not be visible on the surface—will probably distract the Soviet leadership from foreign policy. This could result in temporary reversals on specific issues, or unexplained periods of indecision—such as occurred during the US Secretary of State's October 1987 visit to Moscow in the midst of the Yel'tsin crisis—when the Soviet leadership failed to set a date for a summit. ▮▮▮

vi

SYMPOSIUM ON
································

RONALD REAGAN

★

INTELLIGENCE

AND THE END OF THE

COLD WAR

RONALD REAGAN
PRESIDENTIAL LIBRARY

SIMI VALLEY, CALIFORNIA

Nᴏᴠᴇᴍʙᴇʀ 2, 2011
12:30 - 5:30 P.M.

12:30–12:35	Welcome & Introduction of Keynote	Duke Blackwood *Director, Reagan Library*
12:35–1:15	Keynote Address – The Role of Intelligence in the Policymaking Process	Ken Adelman *Former Director, ACDA*
1:15–1:20	Introduction of Featured Speaker	Peter Clement, *CIA*
1:20–1:45	Featured Speaker	Oleg Kalugin *Former General, Soviet KGB*
1:45–2:00	Break	
2:00–3:15	Panel #1 – Reagan's Use of Intelligence, an Analyst Perspective	Nick Dujmovic *(chair)* Douglas MacEachin Bruce Berkowitz David Lodge Adm. Bobby Inman
3:15–3:30	Break	
3:30–5:00	Panel #2 – Intelligence and the End of the Cold War, A Policy Perspective	Peter Clement *(chair)* Mary Sarotte, *USC* Greg Treverton, *RAND* David Holloway, *Stanford* Martin Anderson, *Hoover Institution* Annelise Anderson, *Hoover Institution*
5:00–5:15	Presentation of Awards & Closing Remarks	Duke Blackwood Joe Lambert, *CIA*
5:30–7:00	Reception	

KENNETH ADELMAN

*Former Director, Arms Control
and Disarmament Agency*

During the Reagan Administration, Ken Adelman was a U.S. Ambassador to the United Nations for two-and a half years and then Director of the U.S. Arms Control & Disarmament Agency for nearly five years. He accompanied President Ronald Reagan on his superpower summits with Soviet General Secretary Mikhail Gorbachev. Along with his wife Carol, Adelman conducts leadership training for top executives in Movers and Shakespeares, which draws leadership lessons from Shakespeare. He began teaching Shakespeare in 1977 at Georgetown University, and taught honors students at George Washington University for years. Adelman graduated from Grinnell College in Iowa, majoring in philosophy and religion. He received his Masters (in Foreign Service studies) and Doctorate (in political theory) from Georgetown University. He has written hundreds of articles and is the author (or co-author) of five books, most recently *Shakespeare in Charge: The Bard's Guide to Leading and Succeeding on the Business Stage.*

OLEG KALUGIN

*Former Major General
in the Soviet KGB*

Oleg Danilovich Kalugin is a retired Major General in the Soviet KGB. Born in Leningrad in 1934, his father was an officer in Stalin's NKVD. Oleg Kalugin attended Leningrad State University and was recruited by the KGB for foreign intelligence work, serving in the First Chief Directorate. Undercover as a journalist, he attended Columbia University in New York as a Fulbright Scholar in 1958 and then worked as a Radio Moscow correspondent at the United Nations in New York, conducting espionage and influence operations. From 1965 to 1970, he served as deputy resident and acting chief of the Residency at the Soviet Embassy in Washington, D.C. General Kalugin rose quickly in the First Chief Directorate, becoming the youngest general in the history of the KGB, and eventually he became the head of worldwide foreign counterintelligence. In addition to currently teaching at The Centre for Counterintelligence and Security Studies, Kalugin has taught at Catholic University and lectured throughout the country. He is also chairman of Intercon International, which provides information services for businesses in the former Soviet Union. Since 1998, General Kalugin has been representing in the U.S. the Democracy Foundation, headed by Alexandr Yakolev, a former politburo member and close ally of Mikhail Gorbachev.

ANNELISE ANDERSON

Fellow, Hoover Institution

Annelise Anderson is a research fellow at the Hoover Institution. From 1981 to 1983, she was associate director for economics and government with the US Office of Management and Budget, where she was responsible for the budgets of five cabinet departments and over 40 other agencies. She has also advised the governments of Russia, Romania, and the Republic of Georgia on economic reform. Anderson coauthored *Reagan's Secret War: The Untold Story of His Fight to Save the World from Nuclear Disaster* (2010) with Martin Anderson. She has coedited a number of books, including *Stories in His Own Hand: The Everyday Wisdom of Ronald Reagan* (2007), with Kiron K. Skinner, Martin Anderson, and George Shultz; *Reagan's Path to Victory: The Shaping of Ronald Reagan's Vision: Selected Writing* (2004), with Kiron K. Skinner and Martin Anderson; *Reagan: A Life in Letters* (2004), with Kiron K. Skinner, Martin Anderson, and George Shultz; Reagan *In His Own Voice* (2001), with Kiron K. Skinner and Martin Anderson; and *Reagan, in His Own Hand* (2001), with Kiron K. Skinner and Martin Anderson. The holder of a Ph.D. in business administration from Columbia University, she has been a Hoover fellow since 1983.

MARTIN ANDERSON

*Former Economic Policy
Advisor to President Reagan*

A Hoover Institution fellow since
1971, Anderson served as special
assistant to President Richard Nixon
from 1969 to 1971 and as domestic and economic policy adviser to
President Ronald Reagan from 1981
to 1982. He is also the co-editor of
"Reagan In His Own Hand" (2001)
and "Reagan: A Life in Letters"
(2003), both with co-editors Annelise
Anderson and Kiron Skinner. Martin
Anderson is the Keith and Jan Hurl-
but Fellow at the Hoover Institution,
Stanford University. Born in Lowell,
Massachusetts, August 5, 1936,
son of Ralph and Evelyn Anderson.
A.B. summa cum laude, Dartmouth
College, 1957; M.S. in engineering
and business administration, Thayer
School of Engineering and Tuck
School of Business Administration,
1958; Ph.D. in industrial management, Massachusetts Institute
of Technology, 1962.

PETER CLEMENT

*Deputy Director for Intelligence
for Analytic Programs*

Peter Clement was appointed Deputy
Director for Intelligence for Analytic
Programs in January 2005. Mr. Clement joined the Agency in 1977 and
spent much of his first 25 years
focused on the Soviet Union—in
analytic and management positions,
including Director of the Office of
Russia-Eurasian Analysis and as CIA's
Russia Issue Manager from 1997-
2003. Mr. Clement later was a PDB
briefer for then Vice President Cheney
and NSC Adviser Rice, and subsequently served as the DCI's Repre-
sentative to the U.S. Mission to the
United Nations before assuming his
current duties. Mr. Clement holds a
Ph.D. in Russian history and an MA in
European history, both from Michigan
State University; and a BA in liberal
arts from SUNY-Oswego. He has been
a member of the Council on Foreign
Relations since 2001. Mr. Clement
taught Russian history and politics for
over ten years as an adjunct professor
at local universities, and has published
some ten journal articles and book
chapters on Russia, Central Asia, and
the Cuban missile crisis.

DOUGLAS J. MACEACHIN

*Former Deputy Director of Intelligence,
Central Intelligence Agency*

Douglas MacEachin is a former
Deputy Director of Intelligence at
the Central Intelligence Agency from
March 1993 until June 1995. He
joined the CIA in 1965 and, for the
next 24 years, worked mainly on
research and analysis of Soviet and
European security affairs. He was Director of the Office of Soviet Analysis
from 1984 until March 1989, when
he became Special Assistant to the
Director of Central Intelligence for
Arms Control. Mr. MacEachin holds
baccalaureate and master's degrees
in economics from Miami University
of Ohio. During the period 1964-65,
he was a full-time member of the
faculty there. Before retiring from the
CIA in 1997, Mr. MacEachin was a
CIA Officer-in-Residence at Harvard
University's John F. Kennedy School
of Government.

GREGORY TREVERTON

*Director, RAND Center for
Global Risk and Security*

MARY SAROTTE

*Professor of History and International
Relations, University of Southern California*

Greg Treverton, a senior policy analyst at the RAND Corporation, is director of the RAND Center for Global Risk and Security. He has had several leadership positions at RAND, including as director of the International Security and Defense Policy Center and associate dean of the Pardee RAND Graduate School. Treverton's work at RAND has examined terrorism, intelligence, and law enforcement, as well as new forms of public–private partnership. Treverton has served in government for the first Senate Select Committee on Intelligence, handling Europe for the National Security Council; and, most recently, as vice chair of the National Intelligence Council (1993–1995), overseeing the writing of America's National Intelligence Estimates. Recent RAND publications include *Making Policy in the Shadow of the Future* (2010); *Reorganizing U.S. Domestic Intelligence: Assessing the Options* (2008); *Assessing the Tradecraft of Intelligence Analysis* (with C. Bryan Gabbard, 2008); *Breaking the Failed-State Cycle* (with Marla C. Haims et al., 2008); *War and Escalation in South Asia* (with John E. Peters et al., 2006); and *The Next Steps in Reshaping Intelligence* (2005). *Reshaping National Intelligence for an Age of Information* was published by Cambridge University Press in 2001. Treverton holds an A.B. summa cum laude from Princeton University and an M.P.P. and Ph.D. in economics and politics from Harvard University.

Mary Elise Sarotte's newest book, 1989: *The Struggle to Create Post-Cold War Europe*, appeared with Princeton University Press on the 20th anniversary of the fall of the Berlin Wall. The Financial Times selected it as one of their "Books of the Year" and it has won three prizes: the Robert H. Ferrell Prize of the Society for Historians of American Foreign Relations (SHAFR), for distinguished scholarship on US foreign policy; the German government's Academic Exchange Service (DAAD) Prize for distinguished scholarship in German and European Studies; and the Marshall Shulman Prize of the American Association for the Advancement of Slavic Studies (AAASS, recently renamed ASEES; co-winner). In addition, the book received reviews in Foreign Affairs, The London Review of Books, The New York Review of Books, The New York Times Book Review, Süddeutsche Zeitung, and The Wall Street Journal, among other places. Sarotte's previous publications include the books *Dealing with the Devil*, and *German Military Reform and European Security*, plus a number of scholarly articles. She has also worked as a journalist for

Time, *Die Zeit*, and *The Economist*, and appears as a political commentator on the BBC, CNN International and Sky News. Sarotte earned her B.A. in History and Science at Harvard and her Ph.D. in History at Yale. After graduate school, she served as a White House Fellow, and subsequently joined the faculty of the University of Cambridge. She received tenure there in 2004 and became a member of the Royal Historical Society before returning to the US to teach at USC. Sarotte is a former Humboldt Scholar, a former member of the Institute for Advanced Study in Princeton, and a life member of the Council on Foreign Relations.

DAVID HOLLOWAY

Raymond A. Spruance Professor of International History, Stanford University

David Holloway is the Raymond A. Spruance Professor of International History, a professor of political science, and an FSI senior fellow. He was co-director of CISAC from 1991 to 1997, and director of FSI from 1998 to 2003. His research focuses on the international history of nuclear weapons, on science and technology in the Soviet Union, and on the relationship between international history and international relations theory. His book *Stalin and the Bomb: The Soviet Union and Atomic Energy, 1939-1956* (Yale University Press, 1994) was chosen by the *New York Times Book Review* as one of the 11 best books of 1994, and it won the Vucinich and Shulman prizes of the American Association for the Advancement of Slavic Studies. It has been translated into six languages, most recently into Czech in 2008. Holloway also wrote *The Soviet Union and the Arms Race* (1983) and co-authored *The Reagan Strategic Defense Initiative: Technical, Political and Arms Control Assessment* (1984). He has contributed to the *Bulletin of the Atomic Scientists, Foreign Affairs*, and other scholarly journals. Born in Dublin, Ireland, he received his undergraduate degree in modern languages and literature, and his Ph.D. in social and political sciences, both from Cambridge University.

BRUCE D. BERKOWITZ

Author

Bruce Berkowitz is the author of several books about intelligence and national security. He began his career at the Central Intelligence Agency and has since served in a variety of assignments in the Department of Defense and Intelligence Community. Berkowitz is a frequent contributor to the Wall Street Journal and has published in Foreign Affairs, The National Interest, Foreign Policy, Technology Review, and Issues in Science and Technology, the policy journal of the National Academies of Science and Engineering. He also writes regularly for the International Journal of Intelligence and Counterintelligence, where he is member of the editorial board. Berkowitz received his bachelor's degree from Stetson University and his master's and doctorate at the University of Rochester.

DR. NICHOLAS DUJMOVIC

CIA Historian

Dr. Nicholas Dujmovic has served as a CIA historian since January 2005. He came to the Agency in 1990 as an analyst on the Soviet Union. He has also served as speechwriter for Directors of Central Intelligence John Deutch and George Tenet and was the deputy chief editor of the President's Daily Brief. A frequent contributor to *Studies in Intelligence* and other intelligence journals, Dr. Dujmovic also is the author of *The Grenada Documents: Window on Totalitarianism* (1988) and, under the pen name Charles Lathrop, a quotation book on intelligence, *The Literary Spy* (2004).

DAVID LODGE

CIA Analyst

David Lodge served during the Reagan administration as a "Kremlinologist" and leadership analyst in the CIA Directorate of Intelligence. Throughout his 30-year career with the Agency, he also specialized in coordinating counternarcotics and related counterterrorism analytic and operational programs between the intelligence and law enforcement communities. Since retiring from CIA in 2005, he has worked for Science Applications International Corporation (SAIC), serving as a full-time analysis and writing instructor training new analysts in the CIA University's Sherman Kent School for Intelligence Analysis. Mr. Lodge has a BA Degree in Soviet Studies from Syracuse University and an MA Degree in Soviet Studies from the University of Michigan, and he spent three years as an intelligence specialist in the US Army before joining the Agency.

ADMIRAL BOBBY R. INMAN

Former Deputy Director
Central Intelligence

Admiral Inman graduated from the University of Texas at Austin in 1950, and from the National War College in 1972. He became an adjunct professor at the University of Texas at Austin in 1987. He was appointed as a tenured professor holding the Lyndon B. Johnson Centennial Chair in National Policy in August 2001. He served as Interim Dean of the LBJ School of Public Affairs from 1 January to 31 December 2005 and again from January 2009 to March 2010. Admiral Inman served in the U.S. Navy from November 1951 to July 1982, when he retired with the permanent rank of Admiral. While on active duty he served as Director of the National Security Agency and Deputy Director of Central Intelligence. After retirement from the Navy, he was Chairman and Chief Executive Officer of the Microelectronics and Computer Technology Corporation (MCC) in Austin, Texas for four years and Chairman, President and Chief Executive Officer of Westmark Systems, Inc., a privately owned electronics industry holding company for three years. Admiral Inman also served as Chairman of the Federal Reserve Bank of Dallas from 1987 through 1990.

ACKNOWLEDGMENTS

Berkowitz, Bruce. *U.S. Intelligence Estimates of the Soviet Collapse: Reality and Perception*, International Journal of Intelligence and Counterintelligence, 21:2, 237-250, 28 Feb 2008. Reproduced by permission of Taylor & Francis Group, LLC., http://www.taylorandfrancis.com.

Treverton, Gregory. *What Should We Expect of our Spies?*, Prospect, No. 83, 25 May 2011. Reproduced by permission of New York Times Syndicate.

First Meeting between Ronald Reagan and Mikhail Gorbachev (photo). Reproduced by permission of Corbis Corporation.

Numerous videos, photographs, and other support provided by:

THE RONALD REAGAN PRESIDENTIAL LIBRARY & MUSEUM

40 Presidential Drive
Simi Valley, CA 93065

The complete bibliographic citations for the material provided by the above can be found on the DVD.

Made in the USA
Coppell, TX
19 December 2021

69449645R00044